AAGAARD'S AFRICA

A Hunter Remembers

AAGAARD'S AFRICA

A Hunter Remembers

By Finn Aagaard
Field Editor
NRA Publications

Illustrations by Michael Robert Bloom

A Publication of
The National Rifle Association of America

BOOK SERVICE

Published by the
National Rifle Association of America
1600 Rhode Island Avenue, N.W.
Washington, D.C. 20036

George Martin, Executive Director, NRA Publications
Lourdes Fleckenstein, Dep. Director & NRA Book Service Manager
Joseph B. Roberts, Jr., Editor, NRA Book Service
Michael A. Fay, Manufacturing Director
Harry L. Jaecks, Art Director
Michael R. Bloom, Design Associate

Contents

The Illustrator

The pencil drawings that introduce and complement each chapter of Finn Aagaard's reminiscences of his days in Kenya are the outstanding work of Michael Robert Bloom, Design Associate for NRA Publications.

Mike's inherent talent has been evident since the age of three when he was copying house plans and drawing animals. Educated in Graphic Design but basically self-taught in fine art, his formal art education comes more from instinct and varied life experiences having nothing to do with art; from travel to oceanography, from music to hunting. His favorite subjects are people and animals; his favorite tool the pencil.

"As I progressed through the Aagaard drawings, each improved, the next better than the last." We agree with Mike and proudly present his accomplishments for your enjoyment.

For Berit

For Bert!

Foreword

In Kenya in the 1950s, a traveler driving from Nairobi or Thika towards Garissa on the Tana River would pass a government outpost called Kithemani. A brilliant splash of bougainvillea blossoms on the left of the road marked the entrance to nearby Yatta Ranch. On the right, inside the government compound, there was a small, friendly dive called the Yatta Sports Club. One evening towards the end of 1954, I walked into the clubhouse to join my friend and fellow coffee plantation manager, Peter Davey, who was dating the beautiful Grete Aagaard, soon to become his wife. Seated at the bar with Peter and Grete was a quiet, husky young man with an unruly mop of hair and shadowed eyes.

"Joe," said Grete, "meet my brother, Finn."

We talked and drank a few beers. I learned that Finn had served with the Kenya Regiment, carried a Bren light machine gun for his section and was presently home on leave after extensive foot patrols in the Aberdare Mountains.

Much water has passed under the bridge since that evening, now nearly four decades ago. Peter married Grete Aagaard and the pair embarked on what has been a long and fruitful marriage. Finn and I became firm friends, and camped, hunted and fished all over Kenya in our spare time.

The Seven Forks region of the Tana River, 45 miles beyond the Aagaard family home at Yatta Ranch, was one of our favorite areas. It was, in those days, a wild and unspoiled place, inhabited by elephant, rhino, buffalo, lesser kudu, impala, hippo and crocodile. Mostly we hunted buffalo, learning how to do it as we went along. We also learned how to deal with cantankerous rhino that occasionally appeared on the scene without much warning. A shot or two on the ground in front of them usually took care of the situation, but when that recipe didn't work, there were some tight moments.

I was extremely lucky to have Finn Aagaard as my companion, guide and mentor, especially during those early days. In addition to being a deadly shot with a rifle, and particularly steady and cool at close quarters, Finn is also a fine field naturalist with a strong sense of sympathy and compassion for the land, the wildlife and the people. Although rather reserved by nature he has an unusually broad range of interests, a retentive memory and the ability to impart his knowledge to others.

Finn's strength of character served him well during his courtship of Berit Rindal in the late 1960s. He was determined to make her his wife and, in spite of some obstacles, never wavered from his course. I was proud to be Finn's best man at his wedding, the more so because Finn had held the same office for me when I married my wife, Simonne, some years earlier.

The subject of Finn's and Berit's courtship brings to mind one of the ways she impressed him while on their first safari together. The game shot on the first day's hunt had to be skinned out — and quickly — just at dusk. Finn began the job. Berit watched carefully to see how it was done, then promptly picked up Finn's spare knife and went to work with a will. Finn told me about the incident (I was not with them, at the time). Therefore, I was only momentarily puzzled when, at a later date, Finn said, "Oh, by the way, I seem to be engaged to my zebra skinner."

After a moment's reflection, I was relieved when I realized that he meant Berit, and not his good friend and tracker, Kinuno, and I said so.

Our fledgling safari company, started by Peter Davey and Finn, and which Simonne and I quickly joined, was just beginning to take off at the time of Finn's and Berit's wedding. The Bateleur eagle was spreading its wings. Finn selected the

A HUNTER REMEMBERS

Bateleur as our name and emblem, and it proved to be an appropriate choice. Like that restless bird of prey we covered a lot of ground on our safaris throughout East Africa. From the source of the Nile to the coral coast of the Indian Ocean, and from the Somali border to the south of Tanzania, we shared with our clients the thrills and spills of safari life. Those were good years and Finn quickly built himself a solid reputation as a hunter and guide. In 1977, however, saddened by the way Kenya's elephant and rhino populations were being devastated by commercial poaching, and unsettled by the Kenya government's ban on hunting, Finn and Berit decided to leave the country. With characteristic determination, they overcame many hurdles before settling happily with their three children in the Hill Country of Texas. When I visited them in 1981 I was delighted to find that their present home is in some ways strongly reminiscent of the Aagaard homestead at Yatta Ranch.

It is said that the mark of a man is the approval of his peers. In this regard, Finn Aagaard has never had a problem: Prefect at the Prince of Wales School, Bren gunner in the Kenya Regiment, full member of the East African Professional Hunters Association, and Field Editor for the National Rifle Association's AMERICAN RIFLEMAN and AMERICAN HUNTER magazines; Finn made his mark early and continues to do so.

Joe Cheffings
Bateleur Safaris
Nairobi, Kenya
February 1992

xiii

1

Kenya Hunter

The rhino came down an aisle in the wait-a-bit thorn. He came without the steam engine-like puffing that usually heralds a rhino's approach. He came quickly. He came with deadly intent.

On the trail, Fritz Walter heard branches crackling from behind, turned and squatted down to look under the canopy. And there was the rhino, its tandem horns aimed squarely at his belt buckle, over a ton of havoc on the hoof, bearing down on him from less than 30 feet away.

Fritz rolled backwards into a sitting position, shouldering his Winchester .375 H & H Magnum and flicking the safety off as he moved. He was hardly conscious of the hazy circle of the rifle's thin-rimmed "peep" rear sight, but at its center the white enameled bead foresight glowed like the sun against the rhino's red, mud-plastered hide.

For an eternity the onrushing beast came, straight down the row, its head and horns effectively shielding the rest of its body. At the last moment, though, the head swung almost lazily to one side and the searching bead found a place to settle, between the neck and shoulder. Fritz fired then, and immediately snatched the bolt back to ram another round into the chamber. At the shot the rhino turned aside — just enough. As it went past him, not

1

three steps distant, Fritz slammed a second round into its shoulder. He sent a rather hasty, third shot toward the root of the animal's tail. In turning from Fritz, the rhino inadvertently pointed itself directly at Joe Cheffings, who was in the lead, a little farther up the trail. From my position at the center of our short column I had yelled a warning, but when Joe turned around to face the excitement all he could see was brush and branches falling towards him, so he stuck a .375 "solid" into the middle of the commotion. As he reloaded the rhino's head burst out into the open, so close that Joe just shoved the barrel of his rifle past the horns and fired. Then he stepped aside as the beast staggered by and collapsed a few paces farther on.

Fritz's rhino was cause for more concern than simply the immediate threat of injury. Fritz shot the animal without a license to do so. It was an act that, in colonial Kenya, was held to be in extreme bad taste — unless the circumstances were mightily in the hunter's favor. The game wardens in those days were generally of the opinion that anyone who called himself a hunter should be smart enough, where rhinos were concerned, to stay clear of them; and that if one did get into trouble with a rhino it was almost certainly his own fault, for which he should be held accountable. Fritz, and Joe and I as well, were cleared of any wrongdoing in the matter, but exoneration came only after a long and thorough investigation and personal interviews with the chief game warden. Despite the hurdles that those hearings put me over, I was in complete agreement with the procedure.

For the most part rhino are easier to kill than elephant and seldom require the sort of pounding that a buffalo seems to take in stride. Rather than trying to get away, a well-hit rhino will often just spin itself around in place, allowing the hunter to pour in several more shots and finish the task. In any fairly open country they are easy meat. If one pays attention to the wind and goes quietly he can usually get within close range and kill them with such relative ease that there is really very little sport in open country hunting.

A HUNTER REMEMBERS

Tracking rhino in dense thorn thickets is quite a different game, however, and one that can become decidedly hair-raising. Often enough one will find himself so close that he can hear the rhino chomping on the vegetation long before he can glimpse any part of it. Only then, if he stops to think about it, does the hunter realize that while flight is impossible, the slightest shift in a fickle breeze is likely to bring the monster down on him like a runaway locomotive, crashing through nearly impenetrable brush as if it were straw. Tracking is not the best way to get a record-book trophy, for a hunter can end up having to shoot an inferior specimen just to keep it out of his lap. But tracking is never boring.

National Geographic lectures and the African adventure films to the contrary, rhinos seldom mount a really malicious charge (though the one that came for Fritz convinced us that he meant it). The rhino has keen hearing, with its large, trumpet-shaped ears constantly swivelling around to pick up the faintest whisper of sound, and an excellent sense of smell. But its eyesight is poor and it appears to be extremely short-sighted. Nor is it noted for its quick intelligence. A rhino's characteristic response to a disturbance, real or imagined, is to run in its general direction, making as much noise as possible, in the hope of frightening away the cause, whatever it might be. When that fails, the rhino most often turns aside and flees itself, if that is the correct term, for a departing rhino usually curls its tail over its back and breaks into an unhurried, but mile-devouring, springy trot, characteristic of the species. There are very few things on this earth, it should be understood, from which a rhinoceros needs to *flee*. Nor should rhinos be thought of as lumbering. Despite their size, there is nothing ponderous about them. They are astonishingly agile and fast on their feet and can stop or turn, on a dime, like a cutting horse.

When Joe Cheffings, Fritz Walter and I hunted them, there were rhino enough for everyone. Voi and Tsavo teemed with them. They were plentiful in the game reserves; the Mara and

AAGAARD'S AFRICA

Amboseli, and the rest. They roamed freely along the Athi and Tana Rivers and across the harsh vastness of the Northern Frontier. Had they not been rhinos, they'd have been pests.

That was then. Now, a scant three decades later, the black rhino is near extinction. Its decline is not due to climatic change, or to the pressure exerted by hunting sportsmen, or even to loss of habitat. No, the rhinoceros has been nearly annihilated by poachers, criminals committed to the slaughter of the species for the transient value of rhinoceros horn — poachers in numbers and possessing the firepower (and sometimes the political connections) to overwhelm law enforcement officials. Consequently, it has become nearly impossible to protect the rhino, except in small, heavily guarded areas in the national parks, and on some privately owned ranches both in Africa and Texas.

When I was a young man there were rhinos ...and many times I cursed them in exasperation and wished them in perdition. Now they are almost gone and I am sorry. They added spice and comic relief to life in the bush, and they kept us alert and agile. If the rhinos were actually to disappear, the "Dark Continent" would be grievously diminished by the loss. They were an integral part of the old and uncomplicated Africa in which I grew and was nurtured, a land that was still much as the Creator made it. They belonged there.

2

Kenya, Land Of My Birth

I was born under the Equator in Africa, at Nairobi in what was then the British Colony and Protectorate of Kenya.

The "Protectorate" was a 10-mile deep coastal strip that nominally belonged to the Sultan of Zanzibar. Within it none but the blood-red banner of the sultan, who was descended from the royal house of Oman, could be flown from a flagstaff set in the ground, while Great Britain's crosses of St. George and St. Andrew might be displayed only from buildings. (When Kenya achieved independence in 1963 she ended this quaint anachronism by simply annexing the coastal strip.)

The East African coast has always been under Arab influence. From time almost before recounting Arab *dhows* with their huge, lateen-rigged sails have traded down the coast with the northeast monsoon. Reaching the muggy delta of the great Rufiji River, they would load mangrove poles in the sweltering heat, or — in the old days — take on slaves and ivory in Zanzibar. And then, in late March, when the winds changed to blow from the south, they would scud home to Aden or Muscat or Kuwait. Mangrove poles were a valuable cargo in Arabia and the Persian

AAGAARD'S AFRICA

Gulf, where there exists no native timber suitable for the construction of houses.

The *dhows* would come into the old "Harbor of Mombasa" with banners and pennants flying and drums beating, sailing close under the cannon of Fort Jesus, a classical Portuguese fortress of such immense strength that it was never taken by storm during the turbulent three hundred years when the island on which the town is situated earned the name "Mvita", the "Island of War". They would unload carpets, Arab chests and dates at the Customs House and sneak contraband ashore in canoes. Afterwards they would often be beached at high tide, so their bottoms could be cleaned and given fresh coats of hot animal fat and lime.

Then, filled with cargo for the voyage home, they would slip out of the harbor on the early morning breeze, or if that failed, the crews would have to resort to the oars. I wonder how many people still living have watched a great, deep-water, commercial sailing ship being towed out to sea by her longboats. I have and I treasure the memory.

The graceful, nodding, white sails of Arab *dhows* are still to be seen cutting the horizon off the East African coast during the *kaskazi*, the northeast monsoon. But they are few now and they all have diesel engines.

The coast of Kenya is as paradisiacal as any in the tropics. Miles of white sand beaches are fringed by tall coconut palms dancing to a fresh inshore breeze, while a quarter or half a mile off shore the blue ocean swell froths on the barrier reef, leaving a calm and protected lagoon between the reef and the shore. Shark attacks on bathers are unheard of along this coast.

Beyond the reef there is deep water almost immediately, so that sailfish and marlin may be caught less than a mile offshore. There are wahoo and yellowfin tuna, bonito, rainbow runners and kingfish, flying fish and the swift schools of dolphin fish that feed on them. Porpoises play with the boats and turtles, whale sharks and huge, bat-like manta rays are occasionally

8

seen, while clouds of terns and gulls wheel and swoop, until they suddenly close their wings to dive-bomb seething shoals of skittering bait-fish. At dawn, fleets of lateen-rigged fishing canoes waft out through the breaks in the reefs with the land breeze, and come foaming home in the evening with the full force of the monsoon and the seas behind them.

I love the sea! It remains our greatest untamed wilderness. If I had grown up in a different environment my life would have been involved with sails and lines and rigging, with celestial navigation, coastal cruises and ocean passages; instead of plains and mountains and the thornbush, elephants, deer and elk.

Inland from Kenya's coast is a narrow strip of rain forest, but it quickly gives way to dreary thorn and commiphera scrub that stretches away into the desolate, heat-shimmering distance. This is the dreaded Taru Desert of the caravans, where many a porter succumbed to thirst on the several days' waterless crossing between the brackish springs at Maji ya Chumvi and the transitory waterholes on Maungu Hill. If the latter were dry, as frequently happened, it was another desperate 20-mile march to permanent water at Voi.

Beyond Voi and the Tsavo River the country becomes hilly, with the Athi River and the wall of the Yatta Plateau beyond it to the north and mighty Kilimanjaro visible just across the border in Tanzania to the south. The country is still wooded and grotesque, leafless, elephantine baobab trees with their enormously thick trunks are a characteristic feature. Then the abrupt Ulu Escarpment leads up to the open Kapiti and Athi Plains and beyond to the city of Nairobi, the "place of cold water", lying at 6,000 feet altitude on the edge of the formerly forested highlands of the Kikuyu country. A hundred miles to the north, its glaciers almost bisected by the Equator, rises the jagged black and white fang of 17,000-ft. Mt. Kenya, the ruins of an ancient volcano whose name derives from the Kitui Kamba word for a male ostrich.

The central highlands are cleft by the Great Rift Valley that has its beginnings in the Jordan Valley, runs under the Red Sea, through Ethiopia, Kenya and Tanzania to join its western branch at the head of Lake Nyasa in Malawi, and thence to the Indian Ocean by way of the Shire and lower Zambezi valleys. In Kenya the Rift is generally 1,000 to 2,000 feet deep and 20 to 30 miles broad. Along its bottom runs a string of lakes, both fresh and alkaline, a series of dormant volcanoes, hot springs and steam jets. Both the Dead Sea and the Sea of Galilee are Rift Valley lakes and the fish that Peter was catching when Jesus called him were likely of the same genus, *Tilapia,* as those commonly found in Kenya's lakes and ponds. The western highlands beyond the Rift eventually descend to the thickly populated Nyanza basin and finally to the hot, humid and fertile former kingdom of Buganda, where the Nile tumbles over Ripon Falls and out of Lake Victoria to begin its 3,500-mile journey to the sea.

The northern two-thirds of the country, roughly everything north of Mt. Kenya and the Tana River, consists of a pitiless, arid waste of monotonous thorn scrub, bare earth and stones, dry, sandy watercourses and crenated, rocky hills wavering in the heat haze. It is a land of elephants and dik-dik, of the javelin-horned oryx, the giraffe-necked gerenuk, the fabulous kudu, of lean, fierce, maneless lions, and of wild, hardy, warlike desert tribes. We commonly referred to it as the Northern Frontier District, or the "N.F.D."

Masailand occupies the southern portion of Kenya, stretching from the high, well-watered trans-Mara country in the west through the Loita Hills, across the Rift Valley and on to the dry, dusty plains of Amboseli and Loitokitok close under Kilimanjaro. (About two-thirds of the Masai actually live in Tanzania.) In former times the Masai dominated a vastly larger territory that extended through the central highlands to include the Laikipia plateau to the west of Mt. Kenya and there are records of bands of *morani* (young warriors) raiding all the way down to the coast.

The British reluctantly declared a protectorate over what

10

A HUNTER REMEMBERS

became Kenya in about 1895. They had absolutely no interest in acquiring what was then a howling, god-forsaken wilderness, but they were deeply concerned to forestall German moves in Uganda, for there lay the source of the Nile, the flow of which was vital to British-controlled Egypt. Furthermore, partly as a measure to help suppress the slave trade, they were committed to building a railroad from Mombasa to Lake Victoria through 581 miles of rough country, up and down the walls of the Rift Valley and across a 9,000-ft. mountain range. Inevitably the railway ran at a heavy loss. Troops, supplies, missionaries and Government officials traveled up it to Uganda, but little paid freight came down. Long sections of it ran through apparently unpopulated country in the fertile and healthy highlands, so a policy of encouraging European settlement in this region was instituted for the specific purpose of producing a viable economy to support the railroad.

White settlement got going in about 1903, and was greatly augmented by grants of land to former soldiers after World Wars I and II. Many of the settlers, but by no means the majority, were members (second sons, usually) of the English upper class or of the aristocracy, with little practical knowledge of farming. Harebrained schemes were tried, unknown diseases annihilated herds of imported livestock, drought and swarms of locusts devastated crops and there were many failures. Gradually, however, those who persevered learned how to manage the land and eventually thriving coffee, tea and sisal plantations, prosperous cattle ranches and dairy herds, and fertile farms, growing wheat, corn, pyrethrum and other crops, were established all across the highlands.

In the course of settlement the teeming zebra, wildebeest, hartebeest and other antelopes and gazelles were of necessity practically eliminated from the farming areas. The lions, too, were killed off and the leopards greatly reduced. But, in Masailand and other sparsely settled areas, and on some of the ranches, the great herds survived in their Pleistocene splendor,

11

and the forests and bamboo thickets of Mt. Kenya, the Aberdares and the Mau range gave sanctuary to buffalo, bongo, small-tusked forest elephants, giant forest hogs and large, dark-pelted leopards. Big elephants and rhino ranged all across the N.F.D., through all the vast Tsavo and Galana country and down the length of the Tana to the sea. They were to be found in parts of the coast province, in the outlying districts of Ukambani and in much of Masailand from the border of Tsavo National Park through Amboseli to the Loita Hills and the Mara Game Reserve. Game laws were promulgated from the first, but there were no closed seasons and the bag limits were quite generous. Even up to the mid-1970s, Kenya remained a hunter's paradise.

Large-scale poaching has now almost completely wiped out Kenya's rhino population, leaving only sad remnants in a few heavily-guarded sanctuaries, and has eliminated elephants from much of their former range. But there are still great numbers of buffalo and plains game, and one can still stand on a knoll on the Loita Plains at certain times of the year and encompass several thousand wildebeest and zebra in a single glance.

My father emigrated to Kenya from Norway in 1927 and my mother, his high-school sweetheart, followed two years later. When he got out of college he found that there were no jobs for foresters in all of Scandinavia, and none were available in Canada, either. He was considering going to New Zealand, where openings were said to exist, when he met a Norwegian settler from Kenya who offered him work helping to run a sisal and coffee plantation at Ruiru, some 15 miles from Nairobi. That sounded interesting and, thinking that he could always return to Norway and get back into forestry when the economy improved, he accepted. Of course he never did go back, other than to visit, and remained in Kenya as a planter and rancher for all the rest of his life.

European settlers in the area around my dad's plantation had built a clubhouse where they could gather after each day's work and on weekends to play tennis, hold dances, talk, drink and socialize in general. My father was probably still embarrassed by his school-boy English and in any case had no money for that sort of thing. Instead, he spent his evenings hunting in the sisal. *Agave sisalana*, a relative of the century plant, was grown for its fiber. It was planted in tight double rows about 10 feet apart and, with tall grass and brush growing between the rows, it provided perfect haven for reedbuck and duikers.

My Old Man would kick reedbuck out of their beds and more or less wing-shoot them as they jumped the rows. At first he used a shotgun with buckshot, but found that too easy and so graduated to the rifle. If there is a better way to learn fast, accurate, close-range rifle shooting, I do not know what it might be. My dad soon became quite adept at it. He would try to get them at the top of their leap and told me that, although he might miss with the first shot once in a while, he would always grass his game if given two shots.

His rifle was a 7x57 mm Mauserwerke sporter with a 28-inch barrel. It remained his only rifle throughout most of his active hunting career. How many head of game he killed with it I do not know, but certainly many hundreds, and perhaps a thousand or more, as he was encouraged to provide meat to help feed the large labor force on the plantation.

On weekends he and Harry Heppes, the senior manager, would go farther afield. Once, while my father was still very new in the country, the two of them hunted the Ithanga Hills. Dad came across a large, horse-like antelope, of a species he did not recognize, and shot it. Harry was utterly horrified for Dad had downed a Roan antelope, which even then was strictly protected in Kenya. They cut it up on the spot, and buried the hide and hooves. But my father took the chance of keeping the horns, which hung on our veranda over the living room door for many years thereafter.

They hunted a lot on the open plains as well, taking eland, zebra, wildebeest, kongoni and gazelles at ranges that were perforce sometimes quite long, especially for open sights. Harry

AAGAARD'S AFRICA

Heppes was a South African who had been raised according to the old Boer tradition, whereby a boy was sent out with a rifle and two rounds of ammunition. He was expected to bring back meat or both cartridges, else he risked a licking. It was a harsh schooling, perhaps, but it did teach a fellow to make sure of his aim and to conserve his ammunition. Harry was an extremely fine shot who later represented Kenya at Bisley. One of his favorite tricks was to wait on an anthill until he had two gazelles lined up so that he could drop both with one round. My father swore that he had seen Harry lie down, set the sight on his 6.5x58 mm Mauser (the 6.5x58 mm was originally a military cartridge, used by the Portuguese, that drove a 157-gr. bullet at 2,570 fps) for 600 yards, and nail a little Thomson's gazelle that was walking directly away with its nervous tail going like a windshield wiper.

My father never got that good himself, but by becoming thoroughly familiar with his 7x57 mm and its trajectory he was able to do creditable work with it at quite long range, despite its round-nose, 175-gr. bullet and modest 2,300 fps velocity. The 7mm Mauser bullets loaded in those days had a lot of lead exposed at the tip. They expanded well, but retained enough weight in the shank to penetrate deeply, and were reliable killers on anything up to and including eland, which weigh as much as a moose. I cannot remember the Old Man — or anyone else for that matter — ever complaining of a failure that could honestly be attributed to that load in the 7x57 mm.

Dad never hunted elephant or rhino, and only one buffalo, but he did bag a couple of lions with the Mauser down on the Yatta Plateau. He killed a zebra for bait and tied it to a tree. In those days lions were still considered to be vermin and it was a common practice to build an impenetrable thorn *boma* (enclosure) in which to sit up for them, and to shoot them at night. My Old Man did not do that. He came back at dawn, crawled up over a little rise 50 yards from the bait, found a lion and lioness on it, and took them both with one shot apiece.

A HUNTER REMEMBERS

He started teaching me to shoot with a German-made Diana air rifle when I was four or five years old and I took my first piece of meat, a dove, with that gun. I can still vividly recall the pride and satisfaction I felt in being able to contribute to the family larder as I carried it home. A little later he continued my education with a Winchester Model 67, single-shot .22 rimfire and, at about the same time, he started to let me fire his FN "Browning's Patent" .32 Auto pistol, under close supervision, of course. We were totally ignorant of the need for hearing protection, and that noisy little pistol would leave my ears hurting and ringing for hours. The Browning resided in my father's bedside drawer all through the years when I was growing up, but because I was allowed to shoot it my curiosity about it had been satisfied. I knew what it could do and I realized that it was no toy. Thus I was never tempted to play with it, or even to touch it without permission. I raised my own children the same way with regard to guns. It is by far the best scheme, but it is no longer possible in most urban environments.

3

Guns Of The Settlers

The writings of Hemingway and Robert Ruark might leave the impression that if the white settlers did not harry the game of British East Africa exclusively with Holland & Holland .465 doubles and .416 Rigby magazine rifles, they at the very least had the decency to use a .404 Jeffery, a .318 Westley Richards, a .375 or .300 Hollands' Belted Magnum, or a shockingly big-bored .505 Gibbs.

Unfortunately, it really was not so. Kenya did have more than its share of lords, baronets and belted earls, and even had a noble duke or two, but the great majority of the settlers came from very different backgrounds. They included Boers who, finding South Africa grown too civilized, had taken ship to Mombasa and then trekked inland from the railhead with their ox wagons, soldier-settlers who were given land for service in World War I, men like my father who had the guts to break free and start over, and the adventurers who by their love of excitement and disdain for the restrictions of civilization have always been drawn to the frontiers. They were a hardy and self-reliant breed, stubborn and independent-minded to a fault

AAGAARD'S AFRICA

(Sir Winston Churchill, who visited Kenya when he was Great Britain's Colonial Secretary, remarked that everyone he met seemed to be the leader of his own political party), but they were never boring.

Kenya's settlers had one thing in common — each was chronically short of cash. When the newly-planted coffee trees bore fruit, or when the herds of imported cattle and sheep matured, or when the wheat was harvested, they were rich. But then a two-year drought, or an outbreak of *rinderpest*, or wheat blight, or a swarm of locusts that darkened the sky like the smoke of a brush fire would disdainfully wipe out all their work and their fine plans and they would have to start once again, rebuilding from scratch.

Few of these men were trophy collectors or firearms hobbyists. Their guns were simply tools used to put meat on the table and to protect their crops and livestock, and occasionally their lives. Many of them owned but one centerfire rifle that was expected to do it all. Price, under those circumstances, was an overriding consideration in their choice of such a gun. So was the cost of the ammunition.

My father used to tell, by way of an example, that when Karen Blixen, who later established world-wide renown under the pen name Isak Dinesen, left Kenya, he was given the opportunity to buy her .318 — and at a very reasonable price. He turned it down because the ammunition for that rifle was as expensive as the rifle was cheap and he simply could not afford it (My father wore out the barrel of his 7mm Mauser shooting at game animals, not at paper targets).

Consequently the guns they tended to use were Mauser, Mannlicher-Schoenauer and Lee-Enfield magazine rifles (and, after World War II, Belgian FN Mausers, or Czechoslovakian Brnos, or Swedish Husqvarnas), often in calibers such as 6.5x54 mm, 7mm and 8mm Mauser, 9.3x57 mm and of course .303 British, cartridges that most of us today would consider rather inadequate for the work. A well-known American hunter and

18

A HUNTER REMEMBERS

writer once asked me why anyone would go after elephants with a .303. The answer is because that is what he had. A typical settler might buy his two elephant licenses a year and hope to make a little profit from the sale of the ivory, but he could not justify the expense of an extra, specialized, heavy rifle just for that purpose. Being innocent of ballistic theory, and having read none of the right books, he would go ahead and stick a 215-gr., .303 "solid" into an elephant's ear-hole or lungs and, finding that the creature died, would reckon he had a fair enough gun for hunting elephant.

Around the turn of the 20th century several nations adopted 6.5mm caliber military rifles. Sportsmen tried them on game, and liked their light weight, handiness and lack of recoil. Thus gunmakers such as W.J. Jeffery were soon turning out sporting rifles, based on the Romanian Model 93 or Dutch Model 95 Mannlicher military arms, chambered for the 6.5x53R, a rimmed cartridge that developed some 2,350 fps velocity with 156- or 162-gr. round-nose bullets. With their great sectional densities these long bullets usually gave deep penetration and dependable killing power even on large animals — provided the shots were properly placed.

The 6.5x53R, together with the ballistically similar, but rimless, 6.5x54 mm (introduced as the Greek military cartridge in 1900 and for the Mannlicher-Schoenauer sporting rifle of 1903) quickly became popular with British big game hunters. They tended to refer to both cartridges indiscriminately as the ".256 Mannlicher", or often enough simply as "The Mannlicher".

Some of these men did not hesitate to use their Mannlichers on the largest of African game. Capt. C.H. Stigand, a very experienced African hunter-naturalist and Governor of the Mongalla Province of the Sudan who was killed in a fight with rebellious Dinka tribesmen in 1919, apparently preferred "The Mannlicher" to anything else, even for elephant.

Stigand did recommend having a heavy caliber double rifle along when hunting dangerous game, provided one had an

19

absolutely reliable gunbearer who could be counted on to stand and hand it to him in the event of a charge.

"Otherwise," he wrote, "I have then found it best to trust entirely to a magazine small bore, as with such a rifle you practically always have a cartridge ready, whilst with a double bore you generally expend both cartridges...and then a critical delay takes place while the gun is reloaded.

"For elephants," he continued, "I sometimes take the big bore from the man carrying it, when the animals are located, and advance with a rifle in either hand, subsequently resting the big bore against a bush whilst I fire with the small bore."

The best known exponent of the small bore on large game, W.D.M. "Karamoja" Bell, is famous for having taken several hundred elephant with the 7x57 mm Mauser. But he also tried a 6.5mm Mannlicher-Schoenauer for a while and had a long-barreled .256 Mannlicher that had been stocked and sighted for him by Gibbs. This latter he used with soft-nose bullets as a meat gun to feed his numerous following, and to obtain hides for footwear, donkey saddles and for barter.

"And what a deadly weapon it was!" he wrote in *Karamoja Safari*. "I have known it to lay out a score of antelope from one anthill stance...I don't think that even now a better rifle could be found for that particular work...It projected a long heavy bullet at a very respectable speed...and it performed well at long ranges as, for example, on giraffe."

Sir Alfred Pease, a well-to-do Kenya settler whose invitation, it is said, initiated Theodore Roosevelt's African expedition, hunted lions extensively on the Athi plains and wrote *The Book of the Lion* that is still a respected work on the subject. Sir Alfred preferred to use a light, handy rifle and keep a double-barrel, "ball and shot" gun in reserve when hunting lions.

His favorite rifle was, "...a rather short-barreled, five-shot magazine .256 Mannlicher; any apparent deficiency in size of bore and weight of bullet is compensated for, in my opinion, by the ease and rapidity with which it can be manipulated, the little room occupied by ammunition, the flatness of the trajectory and the superiority of its striking energy over some large bores.

"With the .256 I have killed many lions as well as pachyderms, and antelopes from greater kudu downwards.... Facing a ferocious lion I have felt quite comfortable with my .256 Mannlicher in my hand and a 12-bore gun, loaded with big shot, cocked on the ground between my feet."

Quite so, but it should be born in mind that Sir Alfred hunted, for the most part, on open plains.

By the time I was growing up the Mannlicher rifles with their *pendulous* magazines and *en bloc* cartridge clips were about extinct. But Mauser sporters chambered for the 6.5x58 mm Portuguese round, with its 157-gr. bullet at 2,570 fps, were seen often enough, and 6.5x54 mm Mannlicher-Schoenauer carbines and half-stock rifles were still very popular with resident hunters, farmers and ranchers. In fact, as late as 1970, one of the chaps I knew at Juja Farm (where Roosevelt hunted as a guest of his friend William Northrup McMillan) was still using a long-barrel 6.5mm Mannlicher-Schoenauer to bash marauding lions and crop-raiding hippos.

Another chum, best remembered simply as Mike, acquired a Mannlicher-Schoenauer carbine while he was managing a large ranch in the Rift Valley. One of his duties was to shoot a score of Grant's or Thomson's gazelles, or the equivalent in kongoni (Coke's hartebeest), every week. This was a government sanctioned "harvesting" of surplus game, in the true sense of the word. It was not sport, but just an unpleasant and dirty chore to be taken care of as quickly and efficiently as possible. Mike did it at night, shooting by spotlight from an open Land Rover.

Once, while I was spending a few days with him, a couple of newspaper reporters from Nairobi visited the ranch to see this cropping operation. We took them out that night, and the first herd we got into, Mike handed one of them the carbine and told him to have at it. His employer had provided Mike with a lot of old ammunition and the first shot was a hang-fire that went off quite some time after the firing pin had clicked, as the reporter was lowering the butt from his shoulder. The second shot went, as had the first, in the general direction of the moon. Exasperated, Mike grabbed the gun and demonstrated how to do it. The carbine said, *click...boom!* five times in rapid succession and each time it was answered by a thump as another *granti* went down.

"That's the way," Mike explained. "All you have to do is to keep the sights on the animal after you've pulled the trigger until it finally goes off — nothing to it."

But the poor reporter was so unnerved that he flinched wildly every time nonetheless, leaving Mike to shake his head in disbelief at the notion that any man, even a city slicker, would let a little thing like that upset him so.

One of the students at Egerton College, a product of Eton whom we nicknamed "Handsome" — because he *was* good looking, and we did not mean it as a compliment — also had a Mannlicher-Schoenauer, a special-order carbine. It had the usual double-set trigger and open sights, and was also fitted with a scope in European quick-detachable mounts. The scope was mounted very high, so prior to using it one pressed a button on the underside of the stock, whereupon a spring-loaded cheekpiece would jump up to provide a suitably high comb — a seemingly nifty arrangement.

Once when we were out together, Handsome got ready to shoot at an impala at fairly long range. He snapped the scope into place, set the trigger, brought the piece to his shoulder and then realized that he had forgotten to raise the cheekpiece. So he lowered the rifle and pressed the requisite button. The slight vibration as the cheekpiece sprang up into place was enough to jar off the hair trigger and, to everyone's considerable consternation, the gun fired. Whenever I hear of some new and wondrous gadget that is going to revolutionize riflery, I remember Handsome and his marvelous Mannlicher.

One of the other students owned a vintage 8x56 mm

A HUNTER REMEMBERS

Mannlicher-Schoenauer rifle. It used a 200-gr. bullet at a listed 2,200 fps and, to the best of my recollection, it killed the various antelopes as well as anything else, though it was obviously no long range outfit. Mike Williams had a sporterized Mark III Lee-Enfield in .303 British that had been fitted with a decent pistol-grip buttstock. In it he quite often used military 174-gr. full-metal-jacket ammunition that he obtained from the local policeman. Despite the belief that such ammunition is totally unsuited for hunting, it seemed to bring game down quite satisfactorily when the shot was placed at all properly.

Although there must have been quite a few in use, I never came across an 8x57 mm Mauser. The 8x60 mm was quite popular, though. Apart from mine, John Fletcher, also at Egerton, had a Brno in 8x60 and several of my father's friends owned them. One I remember particularly well was a much-used but cared-for English-style Type A Mauser sporter fitted with an express sight with four folding leaves, a single-stage trigger, a magazine floorplate release in the trigger guard bow and a horn fore-end tip — a beautiful rifle. The cartridge was developed to circumvent a ridiculous restriction, part of the Versailles Treaty, on the ownership of 8x57 mm rifles in Germany. An 8x60 reamer, which oddly is only 2 mm longer in the case body than an 8x57 (the neck is 1 mm longer, too, bringing the overall case length to 60 mm), was run into the chamber of an otherwise illegal 8x57 mm sporter, and *presto!*, it became a legal 8x60 mm. For some years after World War I, Mauser produced no sporting rifles in 8x57 mm, chambering them for the slightly better 8x60 mm instead.

The 7mm Mauser was always a well-liked and effective cartridge and the 7x64 mm Brenneke, whose performance is almost identical to that of the .280 Remington, became quite popular in later years. I did not encounter many .30-'06 rifles before I started guiding hunters, but one of my pals used a pre-war Mannlicher-Schoenauer so chambered that bore only a "7.62x63 mm" marking to indicate its caliber. John Buhmiller, the American barrel maker who spent some years hunting in Tanganyika, re-barreled a 9.3mm Mauser to .30-'06 for Peter Preston, a Kenya Regiment buddy of mine who had taken him out after forest elephant in the Aberdare Mountains. With its heavy 26-inch barrel the rifle was no featherweight, but it shot wonderfully well.

While at Egerton College I wandered into the gun store in the nearby town of Nakuru with a Police Reserve pay check burning a hole in my pocket. In the shop, I spotted a dandy little Brno .22 Hornet bolt-action sporter and immediately bought it. Shortly thereafter, Brian Verlaque found a Weaver B4 telescopic sight lying in the grass on Menengai Mountain and, as the rings on it exactly fitted the integral bases on my little Brno, he gave it to me. I had thought it would make a perfect rifle for chasing the *Mau-mau* in the Mau Forest, but though I did carry it on several patrols, I never fired it in anger. Instead I used it for gazelles and impala on the vast Delamere Ranch at Elementaita, where we had permission to hunt. I found it very reliable on those animals and a delight to carry. But at any range past 150 yards the slightest breeze would drift those short little bullets 'way off course, which rather limited its usefulness on the open plains.

Eventually I gave it to Dave Watson-Cook, a fellow Egerton student who was going off to pioneer some virgin land at Mau Narok, on the border of Masailand. There he built himself a couple of mud-and-wattle, thatch-roofed huts to live in, cleared and broke his land, and planted his first crop of wheat. Dave fed himself on bushbuck and duikers taken with the Hornet and when hordes of zebra swarmed into his greening fields he used the little gun to drive them off. How many zebra and waterbuck he killed with it I do not know, but it was several score. He would place his bullet into the neck, or from broadside through the ribs close behind the shoulder into the lungs, after which the zebra might run 50 or 100 yards and then go down. One of Dave's henchmen, a Masai, carried a club with a huge nut from some earth-moving equipment for a head. He was awesomely proficient with that weapon, using it to dispatch a crippled zebra or dispose of any cur dog that came snarling at his heels, with what appeared to be a flick of his wrist.

Dave claimed he lost very few zebra, but did find that RWS and British ICI ammunition gave better penetration than the American stuff, whose bullets were properly designed to set up on small varmints. Later he terminated the depredations of two leopards that were killing his sheep. He sat up for them at night with a spotlight and, when they came by, slipped a Hornet bullet between each pair of glowing eyes. He also killed a buffalo cow with it, though even he admitted that was taking a .22 Hornet a little out of its class. When the buffalo got up out of some brush and went lumbering off directly away from him, he could not resist the temptation and gave it a bullet to the back of the head. The great beast collapsed in mid-stride but lay kicking, so Watson-Cook hurried round in front of it and shot it again in the middle of the forehead and then it was quiet.

Several years later I got another Brno Hornet, but this time I dug around to find out exactly what its bullets achieved and kept notes on its performance. I found that within a 150 yards or so it did a fine job on animals, such as Thomson's gazelle, duickers and steinbuck, that did not weigh much over 60 pounds. It was also adequate for neck shots and broadside shots on impala, Grant's gazelles and other antelopes of up to around 150 pounds live weight, again provided one placed his bullet exactly right and avoided the shoulder bones and any angling shots. I also came to realize that it was simply stupid and irresponsible to try to make a pipsqueek little varmint cartridge work on big game and I stopped doing that.

In fact, most of the settlers did use somewhat more suitable cartridges for the big stuff. The mother of one of my school mates presented his father with a used .425 Westley Richards — because she wanted to keep him and did not like his going after cattle-killing lions at night armed with only a .303. Many years later I acquired that rifle, which I had re-barreled to .458. The original 28-inch barrel was marked "Made for Newland & Tarleton Ltd, Nairobi", one of the very first safari outfitting firms. My friend's father had bored holes through the fore-end and through the genuine horn fore-end tip so that he could clamp a powerful flashlight under the gun for night work.

Many of Kenya's settlers liked the 9x57 mm Mauser, whose ballistics were very close to those of the modern .358 Winchester, and considered it a fair lion gun. The 9.5mm Mannlicher-Schoenauer, often called the .375 M-S, had some following. It used a 270-gr. bullet at only 2,150 fps, in the Kynoch loading. The 10.75x68 mm Mauser, with a 347-gr. bullet at 2,200 fps, also saw some use, despite its frightening lack of penetration, while the 11.2x72 mm had an even worse reputation in that regard and was seldom seen.

Among the best of the family of 9 mm Mauser sporting cartridges was the 9.3x62 mm. Though he later traded it for a .375 H & H, Joe Cheffings, whom I first met upon my return from military service with the Kenya Regiment and who became a boon companion, friend, and partner, was provided by his employer with a 9.3x62 mm FN Mauser. Since Joe and I spent most of our spare time hunting together I had ample chance to see the 9.3x62 at work. The cartridge drove a 285-gr. bullet at 2,360 fps, just a bit better than could be had from a .35 Whelen — which was a wildcat cartridge in those days — even in the hottest handloads. When used in a workman-like manner the 9.3x62 mm was effective, even on buffalo and elephant. The cartridge enjoyed such a good reputation that, after the .375 was established as the minimum caliber, those who already had rifles chambered for the 9.3x62 were allowed to continue to use them.

Of course, there were quality English rifles in use as well. Fritz Walter, who managed the ranch adjacent to ours, was given an old and well-worn Rigby .400/.350 by his employer. It used a rimmed .400 Nitro case necked down to hold a long 310-gr., .35"-caliber bullet, which it shoved along at barely 2,000 fps. Fritz used that .400/.350 on everything, including buffalo, and swore by it. One friend had a Holland & Holland Royal double-barrel .465 Nitro Express, another had a Cogswell & Harrison .375 H & H "magazine" rifle and a third whose father was a fairly affluent lawyer used a William Evans, .450 Nitro Express double, but that was about it among the chaps I hunted with, except for Willie Andersson's big gun.

Willie Andersson, a close friend of my father's, had brought a Husqvarna double rifle out with him from Sweden. The gun was chambered for the 9.3x74R, a ballistic twin to the rimless 9.3x62 mm cartridge. To my father and his buddies it seemed a monstrous great cannon and, compared to their 6.5mm, 7mm and 8mm rifles, I suppose it was. Willie bagged a few buffalo with it, but the first and only time he took it after elephant the tusker he plinked promptly charged him. Willie turned and ran, and did not pause until he was back in camp. Thereafter the Husqvarna was always known as "Willie's elephant gun".

With the publication of the 1958 decree regarding minimum legal calibers for large game, Shaw & Hunter, the famous Nairobi gun store, imported a batch of Winchester Model 70 bolt guns chambered for the .375 H & H. They sold like hot cakes and soon most of my hunting companions had one. They were good guns, too, though not as well finished as some pre-'64 Model 70 *aficionados* would have us believe. In fact they were quite rough and mine had to have the feed ramp smoothed before it would function with round-nosed soft-points such as the 300-gr. Kynoch. Nor was the stock bedding anything to boast about. The recoil lugs were seldom in proper contact with the wood and consequently every single one of these rifles with which I have been familiar has split its stock sooner or later. When that happened, we glued them back together, cross-bolted them with stove bolts or whatever was handy and bedded them in fiberglass from an auto body repair kit. Then they held together rather well.

The .375 H & H quickly became the standard large game cartridge among Kenya's resident hunters. Though popular, the

AAGAARD'S AFRICA

.458 never caught up with it because of the .375's superior versatility. A lot of chaps chose to simplify things by having only one big game rifle, a .375, and using it on everything. For that purpose there is still nothing else that can come close to matching Holland's great old round.

Much else changed around that time. Imperial Chemical Industries ceased the manufacture of their Kynoch brand of centerfire sporting rifle ammunition, thus killing off the whole great array of British sporting cartridges (except for a few such as the .404 Jeffery that were also manufactured on the continent and those that had been adopted by American manufacturers) in one fell swoop. With the exception of the everlasting 7x57 and some others, the old Mauser cartridges also faded from the scene and were replaced by the .30-'06, the .270 Winchester and the 7mm Remington Magnum, with the .300 Winchester Magnum coming on well at the time of the hunting ban. They are fine cartridges, all of them, but the truth is that they are really not all that much better than their Mauser predecessors.

I had the great good fortune to be in the East African game fields in their heyday and thereby the opportunity to see how a great variety of cartridges performed on all manner of beasts. When I think back on it and browse through the journals that I have kept since 1956, one inescapable fact emerges. Within reasonable limits, the choice of cartridge is not all that important. Whether a *gnu* is thumped with a 6.5mm, a 7mm magnum, an 8x60 or a .375 H & H seldom makes a noticeable difference. It will run about as far when shot through the lungs with one as with any of the others. Even today, as it always has been and ever will be, it is not the rifle or its cartridge that matters so much, but rather the skill and knowledge of the rifleman-hunter who is using it.

4

Yatta, A Ranch To Grow Up On

I had little opportunity to hunt big game until 1948. In that year my father purchased a 5,000-acre ranch and sisal plantation atop the Yatta Plateau, 30 miles east of Thika on the Garissa Road. The property had been neglected and the living conditions were somewhat primitive. The house, built of local stone with walls 18 inches thick, was solid and always very cool, but lacked running water. There was a galvanized iron tank rigged to collect rain water from the roof, but it was rusted through, so our water supply was transported by truck in 50-gallon drums from the Athi River, two miles away and 500 feet below us in elevation. My mother soon insisted on having a well drilled and water lines installed, but for the 20 years we lived there we used an outhouse (called a "long-drop" in Kenya) and survived very well without a telephone or electricity. Both the refrigerator and the Tilley pressure-lamps burned kerosene and, while we had no television, there were extensive and well-filled book shelves. We collected our mail from the post office once a week or so — whenever anyone had to go to town.

Dad's ranch lay on the border of the so-called "settled area".

AAGAARD'S AFRICA

Beyond its boundaries stretched a vast region of bush that, because it was infested with the cattle-killing Tse-tse fly, was largely uninhabited. It was full, however, of impala, dik-dik, guinea and spurfowl, and sheltered a fair population of lesser kudu, bushbuck, and leopards, and a few rhino. In the open plains that were part of it, there were kongoni (Coke's hartebeest), zebra and a large herd of eland. Some 25 miles away, in the thick wait-a-bit thorn country around the Seven Forks of the Tana River, were numerous buffalo and rhino, and many elephants. Lions were no longer common on that part of the Yatta, but passed through every now and again as, on rare occasion, did a band of African hunting dogs.

From a financial point of view the property was a disaster. My father bought it when sisal prices were at their highest. Shortly thereafter they collapsed. From then on it was a continual struggle just to make the mortgage payments and he was not clear of debt until shortly before he sold the ranch (to a cooperative society of local people) in 1968. It was great place to live, nonetheless, and any evening, when I had an hour or two free, I could pick up a rifle and walk out of the house to hunt impala or a bird for the pot, or just to watch them.

Sisal is a labor-intensive crop and we employed a large work force drawn from all over the country. Among those who came to tend the fields was a young Mbere, "Kinuno", son of Mbogo (buffalo), whose home lay north of the Tana River not far from the Seven Forks wilderness. As he knew the area well, I recruited Kinuno's services for weekend buffalo hunts and found him not only to be a first class tracker and a fine hunter, but also a solidly reliable chap in every way. We became friends and hunting partners and much later an inseparable team when we took to guiding hunters professionally.

My uncle had two 8x60 mm Mauser sporting rifles, brought back from the campaign against the Italians in Abyssinia during World War II. He gave them to us. One was an "African Model", with a 28-inch barrel and a long fore-end, while the other had

32

A HUNTER REMEMBERS

the more familiar 23.6-inch barrel. My father had shot out the bore of his old 7x57 mm, so he kept the long-barreled rifle and gave me the other one. My rifle's barrel was bored and rifled with .318"-diameter "Infantry" grooves, but the only ammunition available at that time was Czechoslovakian and clearly marked "8x60S", meaning it was loaded with .323"-diameter bullets meant for barrels with the deeper "Spitzer"-type grooves. What to do? I went ahead and used it, of course, and fired hundreds of rounds through that rifle without any ill effects whatsoever until a supply of DWM ammunition, loaded with bullets of the proper diameter, became available. I used the 8x60 with perfect satisfaction from 1948 until 1962, finding its 196-gr. round-nose, soft-point bullet at a listed 2,560 fps to be utterly reliable on zebra and any of the antelope, including bull eland that could weigh up to a ton. It was a fine cartridge, but a .30-'06 exactly fills its spot in my battery today.

Before Fritz Walter replaced him, the ranch adjoining ours was run by Jan Allan, a wiry, dark-complected Norwegian with jet black hair, who had served in the Norwegian resistance during World War II. He had several times parachuted into occupied Norway and, after completing his missions, escaped via neutral Sweden, where just across the border he met an attractive and tomboyish Swedish lassie nick-named Lasse (which in Scandinavia is a boy's name). She still did not know his true name when they became engaged, as he was not permitted to reveal it.

After the war Jan Allan found Norway boring and confining, so he came to Kenya. My father met him and Lasse when they arrived in Nairobi and helped carry the baggage. He was literally staggered by the weight of one box. Jan later opened it for him. It contained two U.S. M1 carbines, a silenced Sten gun, a box of hand grenades, a Colt .45 automatic, several other pistols and revolvers, and assorted ammunition. Aghast, my father asked how he had managed to get it all through Customs. Jan just smiled and replied that they had been taught how to get stuff like that past the Germans and that the technique worked on British Customs officials just as well.

The .45 automatic had a large red "X" cut and painted into both stocks to indicate that, during the war, Jan had carried it loaded and cocked, with the safety on. During the *Mau-mau* unpleasantness that erupted a few years later (a relatively innocuous guerrilla war by modern standards, but dicey enough for any chap who lived with his family on an isolated farm), Jan lent my father his .45 (my mother kept Dad's Browning .32 auto for her protection) and I fired it occasionally. My Old Man did not carry it cocked and locked, nor did he ever have to draw it in anger, but there is no telling how much trouble its presence on his hip averted.

I was attending agricultural college at Njoro at the beginning of "The Emergency". Handguns were in short supply then. One much-envied chap had a massive Colt's New Service revolver, chambered for the .45 Colt cartridge, while I had to make do with a Beretta M35 autoloader. I use the term "make do" advisedly, for the Beretta was a solid little gun that functioned with absolute reliability. It was chambered for .32 ACP, though, so perhaps it is fortunate that I never had to attempt anything serious with it. Nevertheless, the puny round did the job when one farm manager I knew called on it. A young bachelor, he lived with the owner and his family. They were sitting at supper one evening when the house servant brought in the soup. Directly behind him came several terrorists, their machete-like *pangas* at the ready. My acquaintance, who happened to be facing the kitchen, picked up his .32 pistol from its place beside his plate and dropped the two lead "mickey mice" with a shot apiece, whereupon the rest decamped.

Egerton College, situated close under the heavily forested Mau range, was a somewhat unique school at the time. Emergency regulations demanded that we carry our firearms with us at all times, mostly so that they could not be stolen by the *Mau-mau*. I remember well the incredulous outrage dis-

A HUNTER REMEMBERS

played by a chemistry professor, newly out from England, who noticed that I was happily engaged in cleaning my rifle on the back bench of his lab while he droned on about amino acids or something just as absolutely fascinating. He was reduced to totally-shocked, stuttering incoherence, while I thought he was making an awful fuss about nothing.

The entire male student body at Egerton — all 15 of us — was enrolled in the Police Reserve. Whenever a gang of terrorists (or freedom fighters if one prefers — they were in fact both) visited our area, John Toft, the local Assistant Superintendent of Police, would call us out, together with such local farmers as could get away, and we would gleefully drop our studies to harry the "micks" through the Mau Forest. We were a motley crew and our armament was equally so. Besides the normal hunting rifles there was a pump-action .22 rimfire, a couple of sporterized Lee-Enfields, a .22 Hornet and a Sten gun that Toft carried until it jammed on him once too often. One of the more affluent farmers favored a double-barrel .470. The best weapon for this fast, close-range work in thick cover, however, was Mike Hughes's old Winchester Model 97, 12-ga. pump riot gun, loaded with British AAA shells (.203"-diameter, lead pellets, of 12.5 grs. weight) that carried 35 pellets to the ounce. Mike once used it to drop five terrorists, who were busily engaged in shooting at him, with one burst of rapid fire.

The *Mau-mau* used many home-made guns constructed from water pipe with a firing mechanism consisting of a sharpened door-bolt powered by a strip of inner tube. Having no chambers, they worked best with rimmed cartridges such as shotgun shells or the .303 British. The shotgun version was about as effective as any single-shot cylinder-bore gun would be (except that the expended case had to be pried out), while the .303 rifle bullet tumbled wickedly when fired through a half inch pipe. They also had sporting rifles and shotguns taken from farm houses, and later acquired a supply of Lancaster 9mm machine carbines and a few Bren light machine guns by successfully raiding a

35

couple of outlying police stations and looting the arms lockers.

From one gang we recovered a fully engraved, 12-ga. Holland & Holland double, a beautiful Mauserwerke .22 rimfire sporter and a Purdey .318 bolt-action rifle — quite a decent battery! In fact, though, the *Mau-mau* probably inflicted more casualties with their *pangas* than with any other weapons.

During the *Mau-mau* years the white settlers in the Kenya highlands went armed at all times. Normal crime — robberies, burglaries and the like — dropped almost to zero. There were a few accidents, of course, mostly the result of plain, out and out carelessness, like the two fellows who were practicing fast draw with empty pistols against each other on the porch of the Lake Hotel at Naivasha (thus violating the cardinal rule of gun safety). When they were through they reloaded and holstered their guns, and walked towards the lounge. In the doorway one of them suddenly turned and cried, "Draw !" The other chap did so, and put a .45 caliber "hardball" bullet in his partner's middle. The bullet went straight through, though, making a neat hole that the local sawbones patched up quite easily and the injured party was out of the hospital in a week or two. Despite the occasional negligent injury, the presence of an armed populace in Kenya had the dual effect of blunting the "military impact" of the *Mau-mau* and of quelling criminal depredations, perpetrated under the guise of *Mau-mau* activity. At the start of "The Emergency", a sign was placed at a scenic overlook where the highway starts to descend into the Great Rift Valley, warning sightseers against armed terrorists. After an incident in which citizens resisted and routed a terrorist gang in the vicinity, it was replaced by another sign that read, "Terrorists — Beware of Armed Sightseers". I submit that this spirit would go a long way towards alleviating our present crime wave, and further that I would feel very comfortable and secure in an armed society in which people were held strictly accountable for their actions.

In late 1954 my term of service with the Kenya Regiment

ended, and I mustered out and returned to the ranch at Yatta. I hadn't been home long before my sister, Grete, and her fiance, Pete Davey, introduced me to a friend of Pete's, Joe Cheffings. Joe had come out of England a short while previously to work on a coffee plantation at Donyo Sabuk. Joe Cheffings and I hit it off almost from the moment we met, each discovering the other's boundless enthusiasm for the outdoors. Soon we were spending our free time down on the Tana River, hunting buffalo. Joe's battery consisted of a 9.3x62 mm Mauser, a double-barrel .500/.450 of German make and a big Smith & Wesson revolver chambered for .455 Webley cartridges.

One weekend we went to hunt with Jens Hessel, a Dane who had a wheat farm on the edge of the Mt. Kenya forest and who was plagued by buffalo devastating his wheat. Before dawn on the first morning of the hunt we were running through the dew-wet forest with the stinging nettles burning our bare knees, trying to catch up with Stalin, Jens's big German shepherd, who was on a hot trail.

It wasn't long before Stalin's barking announced that a buffalo was at bay and the three of us dashed headlong to reach the spot. As we burst out into the little glade where Stalin was holding her, the buffalo cow flung up her head and glared at us, completely ignoring the frenzied dog. Joe snapped the double to his shoulder and heaved on a trigger, but instead of the expected *boom* all he got was a *click* — a misfire! Jens got off a shot with his 10.75mm Mauser as the buffalo turned to go and I noticed a burst of spray from the damp hide as the bullet struck the front of its shoulder. Then the buffalo was gone, with Stalin after it.

Joe broke the double and extracted the dud cartridge. The primer showed some firing pin indentation, but it was perhaps not quite as deep as it should have been. Both the rifle and the cartridges were old, as the .500/.450 Nitro Express (which in British usage means a .500 Nitro Express case necked down to hold a bullet of nominally .45 caliber) was obsolete even then. Joe shrugged and slipped another cartridge into that barrel.

AAGAARD'S AFRICA

Stalin was barking anew. Jens yelled for us to come on and we started running again. We came to a little game path that seemed to lead towards the commotion and followed it, with Jens about 10 yards in the lead. Suddenly the buffalo appeared, coming back up the path with the dog at its heels. Jens threw a quick shot at it, but the buffalo merely paused momentarily, shaking its head, and then came on. Jens, now in the process of reloading his rifle, stepped backwards off the trail to let the buffalo pass, tripped on a root and fell flat on his back. As it drew level with the spot where Jens lay, the buffalo saw Joe and me and stopped. When it did Joe let fly again, or tried to, getting another *click* for his efforts. I poked the barrel of my .375 H & H past Cheffings's shoulder and fired at the cow and, at the same time, Jens got a shot from where he lay sprawled on the ground. The buffalo appeared to be flung sideways and lay kicking as Joe tried his left barrel. That one went off all right and the buffalo lay still.

Examination revealed that none of Jens's shots with the 10.75x68 mm — using full-metal-jacket bullets, mind you — had got inside. The one fired as the cow came up the trail hit her in the upper lip, shattered on her teeth and ended up as confetti at the back of her throat. The bullet he fired from the ground had exploded on the shoulder blade, blowing out a handful of hide and muscle, but hardly marking the bone. Jens had taken an elephant or two with that cartridge, which used a .423"-diameter bullet, weighing 347 grains, at 2,200 fps muzzle velocity. It was commonly used by African resident hunters, some of whom even liked it. I cannot imagine why anyone would actually *like* the 10.75x68 mm. It was notorious for its lack of penetration and for my money was the least satisfactory cartridge ever devised specifically for large game.

I do not believe that Jens Hessel, who later became a successful professional hunter, ever used a 10.75x68 mm on any sort of game after that morning's brush with the buffalo. Joe took the .500/.450 and his 9.3mm into Nairobi the very next day

38

and traded both of them for a .375 H & H, Winchester Model 70 that served him faithfully on everything from 60-pound Thomson's gazelles to lion, buffalo and elephant.

It would have been illegal to use a dog to bay buffalo in sport hunting, but for control work it was quite legitimate. About 500 buffalo a year were being shot around Mt. Kenya in those days, to keep their numbers in check and to protect crops. When whole herds invaded his wheat at night, Jens used to go after them in an open Land Rover. His wife, Trudi, would stand in the back and work a spotlight while Jens, with the accelerator to the floor, drove right into the stampeding herd and then leaned out to hammer individual animals at point blank range, shooting a double-barrel .500 Nitro Express with one hand and steering with the other. It was somewhat reminiscent of running bison on horseback, and while it may not have qualified as *pukkah* sport, it was undeniably exciting.

My kid sister, Grete, married Peter Davey, a coffee plantation manager from Donyo Sabuk. He really preferred wingshooting and fly-fishing, and later developed into an outstanding wildlife photographer, but my father had given him the long 8x60 Mauser and we did hunt quite a bit of big game together. One afternoon we found 15 eland with about the same number of zebra and a score of giraffe out on an open plain. There was no cover, so with the sun behind him Pete just walked slowly and straight towards a big, gray eland bull that was grazing a little apart from the rest. After a while he got down and crawled. Incredibly, none of the animals paid him any attention. When Pete was within about 150 yards he sat up and shot the bull, worked the bolt and shot it again, and down it went. It was a fat old beast that probably weighed well over 1,500 pounds and it had lion claw scars all down one of its haunches.

Then we discovered that we had only one dull knife and a *panga* between us, so it took us over two hours to skin the eland and cut it up. We filled the trunk of my Standard Vanguard sedan with meat and had to put the rest of it on the back seat and on the floor between the seats. Blood soaked into the carpeting, of course. A week later Nils Andersson borrowed the vehicle to take his new girlfriend on a date, but they had not gone a quarter of a mile before she demanded that he stop the car and let her out. She said it stank.

In 1958 Pete replaced the 8x60 mm with a Czechoslovakian Brno Mauser sporter in 7x57 mm, a delightfully light and sweet-handling rifle that I coveted at the time and which I now own. A few years later a leopard killed two of his calves. He recovered one of the carcasses and hung it in a big fig tree. After some days the cat started feeding on it. Pete drove by that evening and saw two leopards at the bait, a big male up in the tree and a smaller one, probably a female, on the ground. There was no cover between Pete and the tree, just a tangle of brush around its base, so he shot from where he was. The leopard tumbled out of the tree into the brush. Pete approached and circled the thicket, but could see no sign of the leopard and, as it was getting dark, wisely decided to leave it for the night.

Next morning he eased into the brush with a shotgun and soon found the leopard, dead. But the ground and vegetation all around the animal were well disturbed, so it may not have been entirely defunct the previous evening. Pete got quite a shock when he paced out the range and found it to have been 150 yards — an awfully long way to be shooting at a leopard with an iron-sighted rifle. He had hit it a little too far back, through the stomach and the rearmost portions of the lungs, but the 175-gr. soft-nose bullet of the 7x57 mm had done about as well as any other cartridge could have been expected to do under the circumstances. The leopard was a huge tom that, with its stomach full of calf, scaled 240 pounds.

They were good years, those on the Yatta. Joe, Pete and Grete, Fritz Walter, Miles Coverdale, Soren Lindstrom and other friends often came down on weekends. Sometimes we would undertake a serious expedition to the Tana for buffalo, more often we would go out to look for an impala for the pot, or to

A HUNTER REMEMBERS

fish in the river, or to shoot a few birds. Pete and his boss, James Walker, used to organize wonderful shoots for ducks or driven guinea fowl that were great fun and enjoyable social affairs as well, but I have never been much of a wingshooting enthusiast. Instead, I would let the dogs tree a bunch of guineas, then endeavor to bag a couple with a Smith & Wesson K-22 revolver.

One Sunday Fritz, Joe and I were out enjoying the afternoon when we spotted a bunch of guinea fowl scratching around in the dust just over a low rise. We had but one shotgun cartridge left, so I sent Joe to bag a mess of the birds for us. We expected him to sneak up on them and to carefully line them up so as to get three or four heads in his pattern. Instead he ran over the rise waving his arms, got them airborne and then MISSED. He heard about that for a long time afterwards.

Eventually a drug was developed that was effective against the cattle disease spread by the Tse-tse fly. The country beyond the ranch gradually filled with people who cleared the land, planted crops and drove the game away. But there were still as many impala, kudu, leopard and bushbuck on the ranch when we sold it as had been there when we first came to it and, in addition, there were several rhino that took refuge with us from the surrounding settlement. No doubt it is all gone now but, as I never went back, it still lives in my memory the way it was.

5

Buffalo And Wild Honey

The entire adult male population of Thabu and its environs, numbering perhaps twenty all told, were happily and gloriously drunk when Joe Cheffings and I pulled in after half a day's drive over the rough, dusty and ofttimes hardly discernable track from Emali on the Mombasa road. It was the equivalent of winter here just south of the Equator, with overcast skies and cool days. The long rainy season had ended only a few weeks previously and now it was the season to harvest the wild honey.

Honey is a valuable and sought after commodity out in the thorn-brush country, where the Kamba people live much as they have always done. The women till parched patches of corn, millet and beans in little *shambas* scratched out of the scrub; the boys and youths herd goats and a few small, humpbacked cattle; chickens scratch in the yards of homesteads where several grass-thatched, mud-and-wattle huts (always delightfully cool inside) and storage bins are surrounded by a thorn fence; and the men — well, the men do that which is proper for men to do. They order and supervise. They clear the brush for a new *shamba*

43

when necessary and burn charcoal for sale in the cities where firewood is unobtainable. They go off to the cities and farms and plantations to seek wages when they have to. They "poach" an impala or a duiker or an eland from time to time with their poisoned arrows. They get together to talk and trade and settle disputes and arrange marriages. They collect the wild honey. And they drink the beer that the women brew.

The beer may be brewed from the home-grown grains or from store-bought sugar. It is thick and evil-smelling and, if drunk fresh enough, is said to continue to ferment inside the imbiber and to keep him lit up for hours or days. The best beer of all, though, is brewed from honey. African honey bees, like most of their kin, usually nest in hollow trees. The tribesmen do not domesticate them, but do provide them with hives by suspending three-foot long sections of hollowed-out logs from branches of suitable trees out in the woods. At the proper time they stultify the bees with smoke, lower the hive to the ground and remove the combs, honey, grubs and all. Bees crawl all over them, but as long as they remain calm and move slowly they sustain remarkably few stings. Natural nests are tackled similarly, except that they normally have to chop a hole to reach the honey. It is, by the way, a heinous crime to rob another chap's hive, one that is regarded in the same light as horse-stealing was in the Old West, and which may bring similar retribution. It simply is not done. Natural nests are free to whoever finds them, of course.

We were looking for a man named Musyoka, who had been with us when we had hunted rhino in this district several years previously, and who had impressed us with his knowledge of the country and the movements of the local game populations. When we finally got it through to him that we wanted him to come with us and help us find buffalo, he mumbled his assent, and seeing no need for any further preparation (he already had his blanket wrapped around him), climbed forthwith into the back of the old short-wheelbase Land Rover. We drove the dozen miles down to the Athi River and camped under a large, shady tree on its bank. Joe and I put up a fly-sheet to ward off the dew, set up our cots and mosquito nets under it, placed a folding table and two chairs outside while Musyoka built a fire, and camp was made. For our supper, I used my little Brno .22 rifle to shoot three grouse-like, yellow-throated francolins.

The first morning we explored upstream on foot. The land below Thabu, at that time unpopulated, ran down to the river in a series of big, rounded ridges and consisted of fairly open woodland interspersed with areas of tight, thorny brush. The coarse grass had largely been burned off, leaving the ground carpeted with the bright green new shoots only a few inches high. Visibility was quite good, except in the thick patches. There were herds of impala, numerous waterbuck along the river, hundreds of guinea fowl and francolins everywhere, many buffalo, some elephants and, for which we were thankful, only a few rhinos. Altogether, it was a delightful country to hunt.

We saw no big herds of buffalo, but tracked two bulls up from the river until, about midday, we lost the spoor. Musyoka complained that an ugly sore on his ankle hurt too much for this sort of hunting. He suggested that we enlist Kimuli, a fellow tribesman, to help with the tracking while he stayed to look after camp. Besides, he was out of snuff and we had failed to provide him with any, as was proper and expected. We spun a coin, with the result that Joe drove to Thabu to collect snuff and Kimuli, while I took a bath on a sandbar in the river and got supper ready. (The few crocodiles left in the Athi after the hammering they had received from hide hunters in the late '40s did not bother people very much.)

Shortly after dawn the next morning we found where a herd of buffalo had drunk during the night and followed them up. After about a mile we spotted them moving slowly up along the next ridge. Through binoculars we caught a glimpse of a very large beast whose horns looked promising indeed. We initiated a fast approach to intercept them, but as we worked our way through the brush in the valley between the ridges, a gray form stirred in a thicket to our left. Two stout horns stabbed skyward as their owner raised its head to wrap its pointed upper lip around a particularly succulent thorny twig. Rhino! We backed off and made a detour downwind, but had not gone 50 yards before we came on another rhino. As we stood, momentarily nonplussed, Joe suddenly brought his Winchester .375 H & H up into the aim and there, between the two rhino and not 30 steps from us, was a big buffalo bull.

Collaboration having been previously agreed upon, I raised my .375, another Model 70 fitted with a Lyman aperture sight and with its barrel chopped off to 22 inches. Joe fired and, as the buffalo lurched forward, I swung and shot immediately after him. The bull went down. Three shocked rhino went off in various directions snorting their choleric dismay — where the third popped up from I do not know, but there it was — and a long rumble of hooves and a drifting cloud of dust up the ridge announced that the buffalo herd had stampeded as well.

Joe shot the buffalo once more for safety's sake, but it was already done for. His first bullet, a 300-gr. Kynoch soft-point, had broken the upper leg bone and ranged forward through lungs and just under the spine at the front of the chest cavity, where we found the remnants of its jacket. My bullet had gone a bit far forward and had by chance broken the animal's neck. It was a big mature bull and as fat as I can ever remember a buffalo being, with layers of lard around its kidneys and encasing its entrails, but its head was not much. We were able to get the Land Rover right up to it and left little but the guts, skin and bones for the vultures.

Musyoka and Kimuli spent the afternoon cutting the meat up into strips about an inch thick, then hanging it on bushes and bark ropes until the whole camp was festooned with drying flesh. Joe and I took the tenderloins and hung a backstrap in the big tree. There the cool, dry breeze soon formed a crust on it and it kept perfectly for several days. The steaks we cut from it were more delicious every day, as the meat aged, but became smaller and smaller as the crust thickened.

That evening the two Africans were already wrapped in their blankets by the fire, while Joe and I were still reading in our beds by the light of a kerosene lamp when, with a frightful, hair-raising crescendo of snarling grunts, a lioness charged camp, meaning to run us off so that she could appropriate the meat. With their bush-honed instincts Musyoka and Kimuli were on their feet and running for the tree before they were awake, while Joe and I made urgent grabs for the rifles lying beside our cots. I forgot about the mosquito net that was between me and the rifle, pulled it down, and became thoroughly enmeshed in it as the cot tipped and decanted me, struggling helplessly on to the ground on top of the .375. The lioness came on until we could see her in the firelight, but by then everyone was shouting so loudly that she lost her nerve and swerved aside. Joe stepped outside and fired a shot to send her on her way. The rest of the night was peaceful, but I noticed that Musyoka and Kimuli kept the fire well stoked up.

The next couple of days we hunted hard without getting a shot. We saw a lot of buffalo, but either we found no shootable bull or the wind swirled and gave us away. Then as I got up one morning I saw the black silhouettes of three buffalo bulls standing in the silvery ribbon of the river a quarter mile below camp. Joe and I took our rifles and hurried down there to try to ambush them, but they were gone ahead of us. With Kimuli we followed their tracks and found that they had joined up with a herd. Some while later we heard a metallic tapping sound, and then came upon a father and son team of honey gatherers who were rapping on likely trees with their *pangas* (machetes) trying to find wild swarms of bees (the sound irritates the bees and they fly to investigate, thus giving away the location of the hive).

Eventually we caught up with the buffalo where they were bedded down in thick brush, but before we could get a clear shot at a bull some of the cows spotted us and away they went.

AAGAARD'S AFRICA

When we got back to camp we found the honey gatherers there, visiting with Musyoka and roasting buffalo meat over the fire. They said that they had come upon, but had not disturbed, another bunch of buffalo and the son, a cheerful and willing youth, offered to lead us to them.

The buffalo were not where the honey hunters had left them. As we began to try to unravel the spoor, Kimuli stopped and pointed to a flock of tick-birds (red-billed oxpeckers, members of the starling family) that were flying past. As we watched they wheeled and descended into a patch of brush.

"That is where the buffalo are," he declared confidently.

We sneaked into the thicket and presently Kimuli whispered that he could see them. About 25 yards away across a little clearing we could make out a bull lying down. It had wide, heavy bosses and what appeared to be a good length of horn, and Joe decided to take it. There was a bush obscuring its shoulder and neck so Joe moved in closer, until the animal suddenly stood up. Joe fired, the buffalo lunged forward out of sight and then a second later it reappeared, coming back the other way. Joe thumped it again and it fell.

He was running up to it when another bull appeared slightly to our right coming fast straight towards us with its head high. As his attention was all on the downed beast, Joe did not notice it. An interesting collision seemed imminent, so I shot the incomer in the center of the chest at about 20 paces, whereupon it turned aside and went away with two other bulls so close behind it that I could not shoot it again.

We made sure of Joe's bull and spent a few minutes admiring its horns, that really were very pretty. Then we set about the slightly nasty business of sorting out the wounded one. We were following up one set of running tracks, looking for blood, when we heard a peculiar noise in the thick stuff close ahead. The young honey gatherer scrambled up a tree and reported that he could see the bull. I went up and, through a small opening, was able to see the head of the bull, which was lying down, apparently very sick. I put a bullet where I thought its neck ought to be. It got up, staggered out a few steps, and Joe and I fired together and finished it. I found that my first bullet, one of the notorious flat-pointed "solids" Winchester used to provide, had entered two inches to the right of the sternum and begun to break up almost at once, leaving a piece of its jacket the size of a fingernail outside the rib cage. (This bullet is no longer made, by the way, and the present Winchester "solid" is excellent.) It had put a big hole in one lung and scattered fragments of bone all through it but, with the other lung more or less intact, the bull was still alive, if barely, 15 minutes later. It was a young animal with soft bosses and I had shot it only because it threatened me.

It was dark by the time we got back to camp, so we had to leave most of the meat out 'til we were able to work the Land Rover in to the kills the next morning. Then we found that a lioness (almost certainly our camp visitor) and her cubs had fed on a haunch of one of the bulls, and that hyenas had visited the other, but had taken very little. We took a Land Rover load of meat to Thabu, where Musyoka and Kimuli grandly distributed it among the populace, and another load back to camp. We traded meat for honey with our guests, warmed it in a saucepan, and strained it through a piece of burlap to remove most of the dead bees and pieces of wax. Supper was buffalo steaks, baked beans and bread dripping with aromatic, full-bodied wild honey and we envied no one in the world that night.

Joe was through, but I still had one unfilled buffalo tag. On the last day we drove downstream along a faint and barely passable track, looking for spoor and, finding none, eventually turned inland up a high ridge. From a rocky knoll I spied a herd a mile away and was watching it when Kimuli drew my attention to a lone bull in the valley below us. It was standing, staring in our direction, as if it had heard the Land Rover. It was a big old bruiser and its horns seemed to stick out a long way on either side. Leaving Kimuli to hold its attention, I worked my way carefully down into the valley, using the trees and scrub to cover my approach. Joe, acting as a back up for my stalk, followed a little way behind.

When I reached the open floor of the valley and peered cautiously around the last bush, I saw the bull perhaps 50 yards away. It had its hindquarters backed into the brush and was staring truculently down its big Roman nose at me. From a kneeling position I shouldered the rifle and tried to hold the front sight on the bull's chest, but I was shaking so badly from "buffalo fever" that the bead wobbled all over. Finally it seemed to settle down and I jerked the trigger. Without hesitation the bull came straight at me, but then stumbled and turned aside. I slammed a second bullet into its broad side as it went by and then it was gone in the brush. While I was replenishing my magazine, Joe spotted the buffalo's head looking at us about 100 yards away in the brush and fired at it. The bull dropped and immediately got up again. Now I could discern the line of its back and shot for its shoulder. It fell and did not reappear. We went up the side of the valley until we could look down into the thicket and saw it lying dead.

My first shot had merely broken the left foreleg just below the elbow, but my second had got both lungs and there was lung blood sprayed all over the bushes where it had made its last stand. That bull was a tough, courageous beast indeed and, if its broken leg had not caused it to stumble, I believe it would have carried through its charge. The horns were disappointing, as the bosses were very narrow, but I will always remember that indomitable bull. And in my memory I can still taste that wonderful, dark-brown, wild honey from the buffalo country.

6

Berit

When independence came to Kenya in December of 1963, it was accompanied by an influx of diplomats establishing embassies and by swarms of expatriate experts from the world's "developed countries", presenting the new nation with a farrago of aid schemes, a few of which were actually helpful.

As my parents were then among the longest residing and more senior Norwegian settlers in Kenya, sometime in 1966 the Norwegian ambassador, Inge Rindal, accepted an invitation to visit the ranch. When he came, his family came with him. I noted that his older daughter, Berit, was a lively, friendly and apparently unspoiled girl in her early twenties, and was impressed to learn that she was working as a volunteer at Kenyatta Hospital (not the sort of job one might expect), but otherwise paid her little attention. What was an ambassador's daughter to me?

Some months later Carl Anonsen, who was on a two-year contract to administer a portion of the Norwegian aid program, asked me to accompany him and a few of his friends on a hunt in the Narok district. They qualified as residents and thus were not required to employ a licensed professional guide (I was working on getting my license by then, but had not earned it), but thought it wise to have an experienced chap along.

AAGAARD'S AFRICA

Included in the party were Berit, her mother and her younger brother, Reidar. We camped in a grove of big, yellow-bark, fever trees on the edge of the Loita Plains by the southern Uaso Nyiro River, at an elevation of about 6,000 feet. This country is always cool and windy, and now in the month of July, the equivalent of winter south of the Equator, it was overcast and, according to my diary, "damn cold".

That evening I took the Rindals out in my old short wheelbase Land Rover that had a canvas roof but no side curtains. We stood on a quartz-covered knoll in a chill breeze and watched Reidar stalk a Thomson's gazelle buck on the plain below until Berit's teeth started to chatter, when I insisted that she take my safari jacket. Eventually Reidar got his buck, so we gutted it, put it in the back of the "Rover", and drove back to camp. Mrs. Rindal and Reidar were in front with me, while Berit sat in the back singing happily to herself. I looked around and saw that she was holding her hands inside the body cavity of the gazelle to keep them warm.

Next morning we found a small bunch of zebra. I parked the Land Rover half a mile away out of sight, then Reidar and I stalked them in the cover of some light brush. He dropped a stallion very neatly with my 7x64 mm Mauser. I fetched the car and, after the obligatory photos had been taken, started to skin the animal. We had no trackers or any other help with us, but I did have two knives, so flung one of them down rather ostentatiously in the hope that Reidar might take the hint and give me a hand.

Berit picked it up instead and set to work immediately. She got the hang of it very quickly and contributed usefully towards getting the chore done. Then back in camp she spent several hours scraping the hide clean of fat and flesh before we salted it, and I began to regard this girl with some interest.

Anonsen organized another outing in August. This time we camped in the Rift Valley near Suswa. It was picture-book Africa, a golden, short-grass savannah sprinkled with tall,

A HUNTER REMEMBERS

flat-topped thorn trees and dotted with gazelles, zebra and more long-faced, doltish-looking Coke's hartebeests than were to be found anywhere else. Round, bald-pated Suswa, the "Red Mountain", loomed over the camp, while Longonot's perfect volcanic cone punctuated the northern horizon and the long, dark western wall of the Rift formed a backdrop to the southwest. In one small valley that an errant shower had greened we found a herd of nearly 200 eland, including a massive, dark gray, old bull with but one horn.

The Thomson's gazelles were dropping their young and we came across one mother who was desperately trying to save her fawn from a hungry silver-backed jackal. She jinked this way and that, endeavoring to keep between the predator and her days-old offspring until, inevitably, the jackal got by her on a turn and rolled the fawn over in a cloud of dust. That should have been the end of a commonplace little wilderness drama, but the jackal was unable to stop and overshot its quarry. The fawn was back on its feet in an instant and its plucky mother had it covered before the jackal could turn around. Then another female tommy joined in, and although the chase eventually went over a distant rise, the jackal was obviously tiring and I do not believe it caught its dinner that afternoon.

I began to teach Berit to shoot with my .22 and then one evening she asked if I would let her drive the Land Rover around camp, just to feel what it was like. Next morning I got into the middle seat and told her, "Drive!" She drove it all the rest of the hunt, flattening thorn brush in great style and double-clutching on the non-synchromesh gears as if she had done it for years.

I wrote in my diary, "Berit brought a cake and a mess of cookies she had baked, and contributed a case of Tuborg beer and a bottle of whiskey (which she does not touch). She helped skin another zebra, pitched in cheerfully to do her share and more of the chores, never complained, showed genuine interest in the animals, people and the country, and enjoyed herself tremendously. The only time we could shock her was when she found out I am 12½ years her senior.

"She is going back to Norway to qualify as an occupational therapist. I should have kept this one, but don't expect that in this frustrating day and age I could get away with abducting an ambassador's daughter."

I doubted that I would ever see her again, but wrote her a couple of casual letters anyway, describing some safari incidents. As it turned out, she was able to return to Kenya the next summer, so I invited her on an elephant hunt.

Jim Clifton, an American volunteer with the Peace Corps who had stayed on an extra year to teach school at Kangundo, near Machakos in the Kamba country, and I had agreed to join forces to hunt elephant, sharing the cost of the licenses and dividing the profits (if any) from the sale of the ivory equally. He was rather startled, and a little doubtful, to see Berit in the Land Rover when we picked him up, but said nothing.

We drove down to Mitito Andei, the "Place of the Vultures", and camped under a huge tree on a bluff overlooking a sandy beach on the Athi River, across from Tsavo National Park.

The plan was to first fill my elephant license and, if any time remained, to look for a buffalo for Jim, as we could not afford to buy a second elephant tag until we had sold the ivory from the first one. On the second day we caught up with a group of five bulls and I whacked the biggest through the lungs with the .458. As it started to run Jim spined it and it came down lying upright on its belly, making it a lot easier to chop the tusks out.

While Kinuno and Nzioka, a Kamba tribesman who had worked for Jan and Lasse Allan and whom I employed afterward as cook and camp manager, were engaged with that task, the rest of us removed a foot and started to skin out the ears for the fine leather they yield. I don't know of anything more frustrating to skin than an elephant's ear. Out towards the edges it consists of nothing but two thin pieces of skin back to back, with no flesh at all between them, and in trying to avoid cutting through one side, one almost invariably makes a hole in the other. Berit became so wound up that every once in a while she would have to stab her knife furiously into the thick muscle at the base of the ear, and then run around shouting and clapping her hands to put up the swarms of vultures that were already weighing down the branches of nearby trees like dark, macabre fruit.

That evening Jim retired early to bed in the tent he and I shared in order to read Bertrand Russell's fascinating work, *The History Of Western Philosophy*, or so he said. Berit and I sat by the flickering fire talking and listening to the swish and chuckle of the river and the distant whooping of a hyena. Then our eyes met, the conversation faltered and all at once we were in each others' arms. (When I claim she made eyes at me, she retorts that I could not have known that unless I had been looking at her.)

The rest of the hunt was spent looking for buffalo. We had two days with a large herd in thick brush along the river, but never managed to arrange a clear shot at a decent trophy. The last morning we tracked four bulls up from a waterhole that lay well inland from the river, and had just spotted them feeding along on the next little ridge when a blasted rhino burst chuffing and snorting out of the brush close behind us. I grabbed Berit's arm and swung her unceremoniously off the trail, while Kinuno and Jim faded into the shrubbery also. The rhino charged past and continued the way it was pointed, wheezing its choleric bewilderment, but the commotion had caught the attention of the buffalo, who were now staring suspiciously in our direction.

I decided that Berit and I would stand there to hold their attention, while Jim and Kinuno ducked out of sight and attempted to stalk within range. At long last, just as the buffalo seemed to be about to move off, Jim stood up beside a bush and fired. I heard the .458 soft-nose strike, but the bull wheeled around and went out of sight with the others.

We found a few spots of blood. I put Berit up a tree, and then Kinuno, Jim and I started tracking the cripple, going very slowly and cautiously checking out every likely ambush spot. But the bull stayed with its companions and the blood trail gradually slackened until it petered out altogether. The .458 rifle Jim had hired was shooting six inches high with the sight at its lowest setting and, in the excitement of the rhino nonsense and the tense stalk, he had forgotten to allow for that. It eventually became obvious that we were not going to catch up with the buffalo, which had apparently suffered only a superficial wound. So around noon I told Jim that I was going to go back to find Berit. I suggested that he and Kinuno should follow the tracks until they crossed a road that lay ahead, while Berit and I walked out to the Land Rover and drove it around to meet them.

The terrain sloped gradually down to the river and it was impossible to get lost, in the large sense. Finding one particular tree among thousands of others was quite another matter and the only way I could accomplish it was by following our tracks back. It took a while, but in the end I stood under the tree and Berit was not in it. When I shouted in a panic, she replied calmly from another roost 50 yards away. After five hours alone in a tree in the midst of a howling wilderness she merely remarked that she was quite glad to see me and very glad that she was not a monkey. Then she mentioned, however casually, that the tree I chose for her had not been as good as the one she picked. I should have been warned right then, shouldn't I?

Between times we celebrated my 35th birthday with Berit's cake, Jim's home-brewed spaghetti and a bottle of good chianti. We talked about every subject under the sun and laughed a lot. One afternoon, driving down the rutted track from Mitito Andei, where we had replenished our provisions, I told Berit to step on it and drive as fast as she liked, as a relief from the boringly slow pace we normally adopted so as to be able to spot game or spoor. We flew down the road, bouncing over the bumps like a secretary bird trying to take off and when anguished shouts from Jim and Kinuno informed us that we had broken two bottles of beer, we merely roared with laughter.

In 1960, while I was a member, the Kenya Regiment Rifle Team won the East Africa championships and, in commemoration, posed for a team photograph. That's me standing in the back row, first man on the left.

For most jobs, Kenya's settlers were limited to the tools at hand. That's why, when lions prowled, my Dad took up his trusted 7 mm Mauser and used it to end their marauding; taking two shots to down this pair.

The 7x57 mm was, and is, a workhorse. My brother-in-law, Pete Davey, traded an 8x60 Mauser for a 7 mm Brno sporter. When this picture was made, he had just used the Brno to put down a calf-killing leopard. Later, Joe Cheffings used it to end a tiff with a rhino. Later still, Pete sold the rifle to me and, to this very day, I own it.

This is Yatta as I remember it, with my family gathered on the veranda; my Dad, just relaxing, my Mom with her tea, a lady visitor whose name is long forgotten and me being, as usual, very scholarly.

Berit on a most memorable day — August 16, 1967 — the day she agreed to become my wife. The tusks weighed a total 112 pounds and, when sold on the now, long-gone ivory market, paid the cost of the safari.

In one of the finer adventures of our youth, Pete Davey used an 8x60 mm Mauser that my Dad gave him to bag a 1,500-pound eland. To get it home, we skinned the animal, butchered the carcass and loaded it into the back seat of **my car**. One need not go into great detail concerning the effect of that operation on the upholstery and carpets.

In Kenya, "vacation" usually means "camping". On a 1975 family outing to Suswa, an extinct volcano in the Rift Valley, Berit had just learned that she was carrying our daughter, Marit.

Not all huntresses answer to "Diana". Berit was expecting in 1975 when she stalked and made a one-shot kill on an impala ram, for the pot, noting only that "crawling while pregnant is awkward".

There are creatures with which I will not share space and a cobra is one of them. A staff member at Juja Farm complained about a snake — 6½ feet of snake — that lived on our porch until Berit and I caught up with him.

My Dad bought this house at Yatta in 1948. Later, Berit and I stayed there until we found a place of our own. Yatta had neither plumbing nor electricity, but it was a great place to live, nonetheless.

Of Africa's dangerous game, buffalo are arguably the most challenging. Tough, wily, tenacious of life and renown for carrying the fight to the hunter, buffalo are sufficient test for any nimrod's skill and daring.

Early in 1969 Berit, Joe Cheffings (r.) and I paid a visit to Uganda. While we were waiting for the Nile Ferry at Paraa, someone snapped this photograph, one of very few of the three of us together.

I offered a knife so that Reidar Rindal (in the plaid shirt) could use it to help skin a zebra. Instead his sister, Berit (with her back to the camera), picked it up and went to work. That's when I decided I'd better keep her.

A HUNTER REMEMBERS

Another evening, after giving up on the large buffalo herd, we had a long, wonderful walk back to the car in the smokey twilight with the evening star hanging incandescent over a grotesquely gargantuan baobab tree with its leafless limbs and enormously bloated trunk. We chased the guinea fowl to make them fly, the giraffe to see them run in slow motion and the impala to watch them leap. We shouted insults at the rhino to make them charge (which they did not do), and revelled in the wonderfully fresh, cool mornings with Kilimanjaro floating pink and white over the Chuylu Hills as we drove out from camp before each day's dawn.

We worked hard enough that a beer tasted awfully good at the end of the day; the nights were cold, and Berit looked marvelous in my big old army jacket by the fire in the evening. When Jim retired to the tent with his book like a gentleman, Berit and I walked hand in hand on the beach in the moonlight, and left crazy tracks in the sand amongst the elephant and rhino spoor. Here I proposed marriage for the first time in my life, promising her no riches, but only that she would be very deeply loved and cherished.

Soon afterwards Berit returned to school in Norway and we courted by mail for 11 months. In retrospect it was a valuable hiatus that allowed us to explain and discuss our thoughts, beliefs, ambitions and feelings more thoroughly and clearly than if we had been together.

I am not a religious man and adhere to no particular denomination, but the best description of what a marriage is about that I know of is the marriage service in the Church of England prayer book. I sent Berit a copy of it and told her that I would keep the vows I made her explicitly, as they expressed exactly what I felt about her.

We were married in the pretty little Anglican church at Kiambu, until death do us part. Berit wore white, with a wreath of myrtle in her hair, as she was entitled to do. In marriage, as in most things that matter, old ways and time-tested values are best.

AAGAARD'S AFRICA

We spent our honeymoon camping in several parks in northern Tanzania, parks that Berit had not visited. We were both booked to help Gordon Harvey conduct a group from the Cincinnati Zoo Society on a photographic safari a few weeks later. It would hardly have done for Berit to have to admit to the clients that she had never even seen the place before while she was driving them down the precipitous track into Ngorongoro Crater, for instance. We camped first at Momella, in a beautiful, lush forest complete with black and white colobus monkeys high up under Mt. Meru. Next we went to Ngorongoro, a fabulous caldera 11½ miles across and 2,000 feet deep, its 102 square-mile floor thronged with wildebeest and zebra, numerous gazelles, packs of hyenas, lions and, in those days, a good number of rhino. We visited the Masai whose village then lay in the crater and introduced Berit to one of the elders with whom I had become friendly. Then on past Olduvai to the Serengeti and so up to the Masai Mara in Kenya, where we found the migration near the Mara River — herd after herd of wildebeest and zebra as far as the eye could see, quite fantastic.

Berit learned to handle the heavy Land Rover station wagon — it had no power steering — both on and off the road, in mud, sand and dust. She practiced approaching animals so as to give her clients the best opportunity for photography, worked hard at identifying birds with the field guide and tried to give sensible answers to all the questions that I, playing the role of the dumbest client, threw at her.

On the way home we had a flat. I told Berit how to change the wheel, then Nzioka, Kinuno and I sat idly by the roadside and watched her do it. The spare rode on top of the hood in front of the windshield and when she was through she had to wrestle the heavy wheel with its eight-ply 7.50x16 tire back up there. She had to be able to do it alone in case the necessity arose when she had a car full of old ladies. We hoped a bus load of tourists would come by to be incredibly shocked by this barbaric African scene, but none did. On the dash was a cup-like plastic ashtray

60

A HUNTER REMEMBERS

that Berit often used as a flower vase. When we got back into the "Rover" to drive on, there was a fresh bouquet of wild flowers in it. Berit started to thank me, but I had to admit that I was not responsible. We turned to look at the others in the rear seat and there was Nzioka almost blushing, with an embarrassed smile on his face.

Berit worked regularly as a guide on photographic tours until the babies started coming and even then often accompanied me on hunting safaris, especially when the client brought his family, as several did. I got her a little short-wheelbase Land Rover in which she could pack the brats and their cots and all the rest of the paraphernalia. On one occasion she and Nzioka went to the open air market in Narok to stock up on vegetables and fruit for the safari. While Nzioka did the bargaining, she wandered around looking at the people, leading Erik by the hand, and carrying two-month old Harald in her arms. The Masai women swarmed around her, chattering and laughing, absolutely fascinated by the white baby. Then one excited old dame started spitting on her and Harald, spraying them both with saliva. Luckily Berit remembered that this was an old-fashioned Masai greeting and blessing, and accepted it as a compliment, which indeed it was. But she gave both boys and herself a thorough scrubbing as soon as they were back in camp.

I had started Berit shooting with a .22, but was in a quandary as to how best to introduce her to big game rifles. The number of firearms one could own was strictly limited, I had no centerfire less powerful than the 7x64 mm Mauser (a ballistic equivalent of the .280 Remington), and as handloading was *verboten* I could not even concoct gentle reduced loads for her. Then, in the Nairobi gun store, I found some 7x64 mm ammo loaded with a 108-gr. flat-nose bullet at 2,770 fps, probably meant for European roe deer, that gave noticeably less recoil than the RWS stuff with the 173-gr. H-mantel bullet that I normally used. With the aid of that stepping stone she quickly graduated to full power loads and learned to handle the 7x64 rather well.

AAGAARD'S AFRICA

Berit's first big game animal was a Thomson's gazelle, taken from the same camp below Suswa in the Rift Valley that we had used with the Anonsen party. She missed the first couple of shots through nervousness, being desperately anxious not to wound, but then settled down and killed a nice buck cleanly. The next day we made a long stalk on a kongoni and, when we could not get closer, Berit dropped it with a good lung shot at 250 paces, shooting from sitting with the aid of crossed sticks. She persuaded Kinuno to teach her how to cape a trophy, turn the ears, split the lips, the whole thing. He was a stern taskmaster, but he taught her well and it was often useful to have an extra skinner in camp when a lot of trophies came in at the same time.

We rented a big stone house overlooking the Ruiru River on Juja Farm, land formerly owned by Theodore Roosevelt's friend, William Northrup McMillan. It was not what one normally thinks of as a farm, but was rather a vast plantation and ranch with thousands of acres under sisal, an orange grove along the river and a thriving cattle and sheep operation. The game populations may have been reduced since Roosevelt hunted it and there were no longer any wildebeest or rhino. But giraffe and gazelles were commonly seen from the house, hippos bellowed hoarsely in the river, and on the plains a mile away were zebra, mobs of kongoni (Coke's hartebeest) and gazelles, with impala and bushbuck in the surrounding brush. Lions moved in from time to time, started eating cattle and had to be sat up for. Shortly after we arrived John Carver, the manager, caught a sheep-killing leopard in a box trap. The game department took it miles away and released it.

There were orange, mandarin, avocado and mango trees around the house, and Berit grew enormous vegetables in what had formerly been a chicken run. The game on the plains was just as wild as Roosevelt had found it to be in 1909. It required careful stalking and often rather long shooting, but almost all the meat on our table was gathered with the rifle. It was a

A HUNTER REMEMBERS

wonderful place to live, though there were serpents in paradise.

One day Kimeu, the laundryman, came in to say that he could do no more ironing on the table on the back porch, as a snake lived in the rolled up tent that lay under it. We prodded the tent, and out shot a long, slender, black cobra. It raised its head and spread its hood menacingly, while it danced around the porch looking for an escape. Suddenly it dived under the kitchen door and slithered into a little alcove where the refrigerator stood. I peered under it, but saw no sign of the snake. Then I remembered that the fridge, an ancient Kelvinator, had a sort of drawer to catch the water when one defrosted it. We moved it to an open window, went outside and opened the drawer with a long stick and, sure enough, there was the cobra coiled up in the bottom. We killed it with some regret, but one can't really have a large venomous snake in the house frightening the help. It was six feet, six inches long, but weighed only three pounds. Later we came across an even larger, shiny, black cobra while hunting along the southern Uaso Nyiro near Narok. It raised several feet of itself off the ground, spread its hood and regarded us calmly, as if to ask, "Are you chaps looking for trouble?"

We backed off a step and replied in plain body language, "No sir, Mr. Cobra, we are not looking for any trouble at all."

The beautiful great snake held us there a few moments longer to ensure that we properly understood our lowly rank and then went regally on its way.

Eventually the English owner of Juja Farm decided that for tax reasons he would live half the year in Kenya and he took over our house. We moved in with my parents for a while and then, in order to be within reach of schools for the kids, we acquired a five-acre plot and built a house on the outskirts of Nairobi. Giraffe sometimes came by there, bushbuck lived along the stream that ran at the bottom of the plot and we could often hear the lions calling in the national park half a mile away. But it was by no means Yatta or Juja Farm and the years we spent there are the last I will live in any sort of town, if I can help it.

7

The Elephant
That Vanished

In Kenya, prior to 1977, a professional hunter's license was officially called an "Assistant's Permit". It entitled the holder to accompany visiting sportsmen and to provide guidance and assistance as they hunted various game animals, as the law required. An Assistant's Permit was not to be had easily. In the first place, an applicant had to have hunted for at least three years on a resident's full license before he would even be considered. Then his file, which contained the game registers he was required to submit every year listing all game animals he had taken *or wounded* and details of any actual or suspected infringements of the game regulations, would be thoroughly examined by members of the department.

The next step was a written examination, mostly on the game laws and regulations of Kenya, and the duties of a professional hunter thereunder. The minimum passing grade was 100%.

Survivors went before a board consisting of the assistant chief game warden, a couple of game rangers and two or three senior professional hunters. These gentlemen would examine and cross-examine the applicant mercilessly until they felt that they had thoroughly probed the depths of his experience and competence and would then make a recommendation to the chief game warden.

A period of apprenticeship under an established professional in order to learn how to organize and run a safari properly might be required. Very often the recommendation would be for the issuance of a restricted permit, allowing the neophyte professional to guide for non-dangerous game and, usually, buffalo. Buffalo were by far the most common of the dangerous game. Bag limits were three or four a year and the licenses were inexpensive. Besides, where buffalo were damaging crops on private land there were no restrictions on hunting them, so most of us had ample experience with buffalo. But quite commonly the board would feel that we needed to prove ourselves a little more on some of the other dangerous game before they would set us completely free.

My partner, Joe Cheffings, and I had reached that stage. Because we had already been running our own outfitting business (mostly photo safaris) for a couple of years, we were excused the apprenticeship requirement, but Joe had to take another lion, and I both a lion and an elephant, before they would lift the restrictions on our permits. We decided to get it done, so booked Hunting Block 26, near Voi, and arranged to hunt Ray Mayer's 100,000-acre ranch in the vicinity at the same time. Ray's property bounded on Tsavo National Park, and the elephant were constantly coming in and destroying his concrete water tanks by standing up on their hind legs with their forequarters and much of their weight resting on the rim of the structure while they endeavored to reach the water with their trunks. Lions killed Ray's cattle with appalling regularity as well, so we were not unwelcome.

Perhaps it would be more accurate to say that we were more welcome than most, for as far as I know no one was ever *unwelcome* at Ray Mayer's. Ray, who was born in Australia, was one of those glorious characters who made colonial Kenya such a marvelous place to live. He had served as a District Commissioner in the military administration of Somalia during World War II. There he kept the peace with the aid of the Somalia Gendarmerie, a unit whose British officers were by all accounts as rare a mob of far-gone eccentrics as one could wish to meet. Ray had an inexhaustible store of humorous tales and had seen far too much of life to take any of it very seriously. He and his wife, Helen, were probably the most hospitable couple I have ever known. A ranch house they built later, near Voi, had no doors whatsoever. Anyone could walk in, and if they did not stay at least a week Ray and Helen were quite disappointed. Thus it was that, accompanied by my wife, Berit, Joe and I made camp half a mile from Ray's house, under Maungu Hill, and then set out to reconnoiter Block 26.

Away down past Kasigau Mountain, where the Mwatate, a smallish stream, crosses the main road through Block 26, we came upon a few local chaps who were burning charcoal for sale as cooking fuel in Mombasa or Nairobi. They said that they heard lions every night and, as it was a nice, uninhabited section of wild country, with a fair population of zebra, eland and hartebeest, that seemed not unlikely. We saw a black serval cat here, which was only the second melanistic serval I had ever come across. There was little elephant sign, though. So Joe and my tracker, Kinuno, came back with a spike camp and hunted lion there for several days, while Berit and I remained at Maungu and looked for elephant on Ray's ranch.

It was toward the end of an exceptionally good rainy season and every twisted, stunted tree and thorny bush in the Taru Desert was frantically engaged in putting several year's growth into a few weeks. The weather was hot and humid, and the normally sere, gray brush was a brilliant, vibrant green and was as impenetrable in places as a Hollywood jungle. All the buffalo, rhino, elephants and warthogs, newly plastered with shiny wet mud, were exactly the same color as the red termite hills.

One evening we came upon a shiny, wet, red elephant bull

ambling along one of the ranch roads. Its ivory appeared quite decent, so that at the then-market value of about $2.85 per pound it would sell for enough to cover the cost of the license and would most likely pay part of the expenses of the safari as well — a matter of some importance to impecunious resident hunters such as ourselves. I trotted after the bull, then ran out to the side until I had a broadside shot. As it was moving I did not essay a brain shot, but instead thumped it with my .458 Magnum close behind the front leg when it stretched it forward in its walking. The elephant immediately spun round and plowed into the brush. I got off a second, very hurried shot as the vegetation closed around it, trying without success for the spine just above the root of the tail. Then it was gone.

As we stood there, listening, Berit suddenly said, "I hear it, it's down! Did you hear that bellowing and gurgling? It's dead, I'm sure of it!"

Almost immediately a frightful clamor broke out, a cacophony of trumpeting and screaming as a mob of elephant deeper in the bush panicked and began stampeding back and forth in total confusion. We waited patiently until at last they moved away and then went in to retrieve our prize.

We could not find it. There was not a drop of blood, but I was able to follow its tracks easily, until we reached the area in which the other terrified jumbos had run back and forth. There, our elephant's tracks were abruptly wiped out. So, from the area of the stampede, we searched in the direction of the elephant's dying bellows until it got too dark, but without success. Still, we weren't discouraged, the shrubbery was so thick that in many places one could pass within 10 yards of an elephant and not see it. We would surely find it on the morrow.

That night it rained hard enough to wash out the tracks and any blood there might have been. We searched all the next day and the day after, and found not a sign of our bull. Now I was seriously worried. Could I have missed it completely? No way! I may not be the world's best shot, but I don't miss a whole elephant at 30 paces. I went over every detail of the hunt again and again in my mind. I could clearly recall the white bead hanging firmly on its chest as the shot went off. As I had pulled a little ahead of the bull before stopping to shoot, the bullet might have angled back towards the rear of the lungs more than I allowed for, but even so it should have been mortal and Berit had heard it die. But that jumbo had vanished without trace, like a puff of smoke, or as if we had dreamed it all. Even the vultures refused to give us a clue.

On the morning of the third day we were hopelessly searching the area one more time before giving it up, when a faint odor struck our noses. Stink ants, I thought. They are common during the rains, and when disturbed give off a stench like carrion. The smell came and went, and then gradually strengthened. We followed it upwind until we came to a strange red termite mound under a big tree. Only it wasn't an anthill, it was our elephant, three days dead, down on its belly and leaning against the tree, which held it upright. I grasped the left tusk, jerked it up and down a few times and then pulled it easily from its socket. But the weight of the head was on the other tusk and eventually we had to chop it free. There were lion tracks all around the elephant and they had been feeding on it behind the ears, where the skin is soft and thin.

Shooting at night was strictly prohibited in normal hunting and rightly so. But the rules did not apply on private land, when crops or livestock were being threatened. Ray knew, from bitter experience, how quickly lions learn that cattle are much easier to catch than zebra and such, and when he heard of our find he gave us a six-volt flashlight and insisted that we should sit up for the lions that night and rid him of the vermin before they started on his cows.

Joe and Kinuno got back from the Mwatate area about noon the same day. They had seen a beautiful big leopard, but no lions. They had heard them the first night and in the distance on the second night, but then no more. Apparently the pride had moved on and they had been unable to make contact with them again. That evening Joe, Kinuno and I left the Land Rover by a road and, following the trail that Berit and I had blazed, walked in half a mile to the elephant. We found a suitable spot to sit about 30 yards from the carcass and cut down a few intervening bushes that we placed in a half circle behind us.

Then we sat down and waited, Kinuno with the flashlight and Joe and I with our Winchester, .375 H & H rifles. Mine, although newly-acquired because I had been without a "three-seven-five" for a while, was a 20-year old Model 70 fitted with a Weaver K2.5 scope that was so ancient that its reticle did not remain centered when the adjustment knobs were turned to zero it. Nevertheless, that old scope was vastly better for any form of night shooting than the iron sights on my .458. Joe had an aperture receiver sight on his well-used Winchester.

The lions came as soon as it was full dark. We heard an odd sort of thumping noise from the elephant. I nudged Joe and then Kinuno, who put the flashlight on. There was a lion on the elephant, tearing at the meat behind the ear. As the light hit it, the lion let go its hold, allowing the elephant's head to thump back down to the ground, then stood up and sprang off the carcass before I could get the sights on it. Darn it — had we blown our chance? We turned the light out and waited again.

Presently we heard quiet padding sounds a few feet behind us. The lion had circled around downwind and stalked us, as if to find out what was causing this business with the light. Now what? Perhaps we should stand up suddenly, whirl, try to catch it in the light and shoot instantly. But the lion was so close that if startled it could be among us long before we had completed the maneuver. We sat tight in tense, frozen immobility. There really was nothing else to do; the lion had the ball. It sniffed a couple of times and then it padded softly away.

Shortly it was tearing at the elephant once more. This time there was a second lion standing on the ground beside the jumbo, but again they leaped away as soon as the light came on.

A HUNTER REMEMBERS

They were both young adult males, sleek, powerful and in fine condition, but almost maneless, as Tsavo lions often are. They were undoubtedly park lions, who had not learned to fear man. Upon reaching maturity they had been driven out of the pride and, finding no unoccupied territory within the park, had perforce to seek their fortunes elsewhere. It was simply unfortunate for them, and a very sad thing, that there was no longer any room for them outside the park either.

The lions came back to the elephant as soon as we switched the light off. This time we gave them a quarter of an hour to get well stuck into it before Joe, who had taken over the flashlight, turned it on again. The one on the elephant sprang up immediately, but then hesitated a second too long. The post in the scope found the center of its chest, directly above the fore leg. At the shot the lion jumped down behind the elephant with a roar, growled and moaned a few moments as it thrashed the bush, then was still.

We knew it was dead, but gave it a few minutes anyway. As we started walking towards the elephant, Joe and Kinuno both heard a sound over to our left and flashed the light in that direction. There was the second lion, moving back towards the elephant carcass. I swung up the .375 and, as the lion passed a gap between two bushes, the reticle settled so beautifully on its shoulder that I had to shoot. The lion grunted and was gone.

Joe was somewhat taken aback. "You shot awfully fast," he said, a bit accusingly.

True. But the sights had looked to be perfectly placed as the gun went off, so it should have been well hit. One can never be absolutely certain of that, though, until he is standing over the beast and has poked it cautiously in the eye with the muzzle of the rifle. Trying to find a lion — and probably a wounded lion at that — in the black of night with a dimming light was going to be interesting, perhaps suicidal.

We climbed up on the elephant and shone the light around, but could not see the lions. The flashlight was fading fast, its

71

battery almost dead. Joe and I looked at each other and voiced the same thought simultaneously. The only sensible thing to do was fetch the Land Rover and use its headlights and spotlight to find our cats. Or else return at first light and hope the hyenas did not find them in the meantime.

We fetched the Land Rover. Kinuno had to hack a lot of brush with his *panga* (machete) to achieve that, but eventually we were able to get the car up to the elephant and, when that was done, quickly found both lions lying within about 20 paces of each other. With some difficulty we heaved them into the vehicle, drove home, woke Berit and watched her astonishment as we dumped a Land Rover-full of lions at her feet.

It may be worth noting that despite having a very large aperture on his receiver sight Joe had not been able to get on to the lions anything like as quickly as I could with the scope. I used Winchester ammo with 270-gr. Power Point bullets, which have always given me excellent results. Two lions with two consecutive shots is not a shabby start to any rifle's career and that .375 went on to become my most favorite "old Betsy". We shared many other little adventures afterwards.

The elephant tusks weighed 66 and 70 pounds, which was fairly respectable even in those days. They more than covered the cost of the license and, by selling the lion skins as well, we about broke even on the hunt. Kinuno and Nzioka rendered the fat from around the lions' internal organs and got a good price for it from members of the Asian community, who regarded it as a specific for rheumatism and other ailments.

This tale has no moral, except perhaps that it is not the trophies that make the hunt. We gained no trophies from it, yet it remains among my more memorable experiences. There is a lion skull on my mantlepiece, but whether it came from one of these lions, or from another that killed one of my own cows not a quarter mile from our house, I no longer remember and it really does not matter. In those days we hunted mostly for the sake of hunting, and that is still the way it is with me.

8

Rifles And Cartridges

It was not until I started guiding them for a living that I realized how thoroughly American hunters had been brainwashed into believing that African game animals are incredibly tough and that hunting them requires far heavier artillery than does hunting their American counterparts. This is purely a fallacy.

Indeed, some African beasts do seem to be more phlegmatic and more resistant to bullet shock than some American animals, but the reverse is also true. Few African antelopes show less reaction to bullet shock than the mountain goat, native to the U.S. and Canadian Rockies, all too often does. A moose can soak up as many poor hits as an eland will. A gut-shot elk will probably run further than any similarly hit zebra, waterbuck or kudu. On the other hand, an impala or a bushbuck, while not so highly-strung or nervously alert as a whitetail deer, will go down just as quickly when well hit with comparable cartridges.

Apart from the bison, which I am not sure can any longer be counted a true game animal, and perhaps the walrus, there is nothing in America that compares with Africa's elephants, rhino

75

and buffalo. But the great brown and grizzly bears seem able to carry at least as much badly-placed lead as African lions and leopards, and a big black bear is no wimp, either.

The truth is that what works on deer, elk, caribou, pronghorn, moose and bear in America will do equally well under like conditions on similar-size game in Africa. The key, as always, is the placement of the shot and the performance of the bullet after impact. To illustrate, Gail Pringle, who accompanied her husband, Alec, and me on a safari for elephant, used a .243 Winchester with factory 100-gr. bullets to drop a good Grant's gazelle at 150 yards with one perfectly-placed shot. There were several fine trophy bucks in the bunch, and they ran only half a mile before settling down again, so Alec followed them up hoping to add his own specimen to the bag. He eventually got a superb trophy buck — even better than Gail's — but because he put the first shot too far back he had to shoot it two or three times with his .300 Weatherby Magnum, something we never let him forget. Power cannot make up for poor bullet placement to any very significant degree.

An animal is killed, or at least falls down, when its muscles cease to receive coherent orders from its brain. This can be accomplished by severing the lines of communication — cutting the spinal cord— or putting the brain out of action, either directly or by shutting off its blood supply. A brain shot is instantly effective, as is a shot to the spine forward of the withers. Hitting the spine farther to the rear paralyzes the hindquarters, anchoring the animal for a *coup de grace*.

Many believe that a neck or brain shot must result in either a clean miss or a clean kill, but that is far from being the case. Both the brain and the spinal column offer small targets surrounded by bone and heavy muscle not immediately vital to life. Miscued attempts at either the brain or the neck can result in an animal escaping with a torn gullet or smashed jaw to die a lingering death. At any but the closest range the heart/lung area offers a more certain, and a far better, target.

A HUNTER REMEMBERS

When shooting for the vital areas apart from the central nervous system, the idea is to induce such profuse bleeding that the blood pressure quickly drops to zero, thus depriving the brain of its essential oxygen. The blood supply to the whole body (except the lungs) is pumped out of the heart through the *aorta*. When this great artery is cut close to the heart, before it has branched much, all blood pressure is gone and delivery of blood to the brain ceases almost immediately. The *venae cavae*, the paired veins that carry the blood from most of the body back to the heart, enter at the top of the heart. The pulmonary arteries and veins arise there also. Thus above the heart is a thick rope of major blood vessels, the severing of any one of which will cause sufficiently copious bleeding to bring an animal down in short order. The same is true of the thin-walled upper chambers of the heart, but the lower portions of it consist of the muscular ventricles, that do the actual pumping. A perforating wound here that does not tear them wide open may bleed comparatively slowly and will sometimes permit an animal to travel an astonishing distance. The lungs are well-supplied with blood, of course, but a shot placed close to where the pulmonary vessels enter them, more or less directly above the heart, will result in much more severe bleeding than one that disrupts only their outer fringes, where the blood vessels are smaller.

Despite some curious beliefs on the subject held by many hunters, the heart is quite a large organ that occupies the center of the chest cavity, with the lungs enveloping it on either side. It is encased in a tough, membranous bag, the *pericardium*, that holds it in place while giving it room to pulsate. In animals that walk on four legs the lower apex of the heart comes down almost to the breast bone, but its vital upper parts, the great blood vessels and the center of the lungs all lie much higher, between a third and one half the depth of the chest up from the brisket. When the animal is standing exactly broadside, one should bring the sights up the front leg until they are almost halfway up on the chest and place the bullet there. It will pass through the shoulder muscles but just behind the actual shoulder joint, and quite likely in the angle formed by the upper leg bone and the shoulder blade, without striking either, though that depends on how the leg is being held at that moment. Alternatively, imagine that the animal has a grapefruit suspended in the center of its chest, above the front legs. Given that a bullet performs as intended, a shot that strikes that imaginary grapefruit will hit the center of the lungs, or the upper chambers of the heart, or the major blood vessels leading to and from it. Such a hit will totally disrupt the circulatory system and the beast, whether African or American, will usually be down well within 50 steps.

The classic American behind-the-shoulder shot, by contrast, tends to get only the rear portion of the lungs, and to pass behind the heart and the great blood vessels. It will kill, but it needs a "soft" bullet — one that will expand very rapidly and induce sufficient bleeding — if it is to kill quickly and such bullets give limited penetration. They can work superbly on broadside shots, but at other angles they may break up on heavy bones and solid shoulder muscles, or fail to get through a couple of feet of grass-packed paunch.

On an African hunt one will usually be hunting a diversity of game that varies considerably in size. It would be rather impractical to use a different load, possibly requiring a different sight setting, for each and every species. Far better to choose one that will surely give sufficient penetration for the largest animal that might be taken with that rifle and use it on all the lesser beasts as well. With the African center-of-the-shoulder-area hold explosive expansion is not a requisite, and a bullet and load that are adequate for an eland will also drop impala very satisfactorily. As a rough rule of thumb, a bullet that will not always exit on a broadside shot is unlikely to have sufficient penetration from other angles to be thoroughly reliable on that size of animal. I have seen failures due to insufficient pene-tration on lion, zebra and buffalo, but I have never experienced an incident in which the failure of the bullet to do its job could honestly be blamed on excessive penetration.

With today's "premium", controlled-expansion bullets one can, to some extent, have his cake and eat it, too. Projectiles such as the Trophy Bonded "Bearclaw", the Swift "A-frame", the all-copper Barnes "X-Bullet" and the famous Nosler "Partition" Bullet are designed to start expanding very easily, but then at some point a partition or a solid copper base prevents further expansion, so that a good length of shank remains to provide sufficient weight for deep penetration. The Trophy Bonded and the Swift have the lead core bonded to the jacket and together with the Barnes they usually retain 90% of their original weight when fully expanded. With the Nosler Partition, on the other hand, the front core tends to shed fragments as secondary missiles, then the wings of the jacket fold in against the shank, so that the bullet presents a small frontal area and will usually give comparable penetration to the others despite retaining an average of only 65% of its original weight. The old RWS "H-Mantel", like the Nosler Partition, has a front end (ahead of a deep fold in the jacket that acts as a partition) that tends to break completely away, leaving the cylindrical rear half to keep boring on like a little "solid". I used that bullet in 173-gr. weight for years in my 7x64 mm and found it to be an extremely reliable performer. That rifle accounted for over 300 head of big game, ranging in size from little Thomson's gazelle to 800-pound Grevy's zebra, with very few failures, and none of those could be blamed on RWS's bullet.

The premium bullets tend to be expensive, though the Noslers are less so than the others, which are to some degree hand-made. Regardless, they are worth it and, when the cost of an African safari is taken into account, the extra assurance they provide is dirt cheap. Federal in particular offers ammunition loaded with Nosler Partition bullets in many calibers and Remington factory ammo for their .416 Magnum uses the Swift A-frame soft-nose bullet.

AAGAARD'S AFRICA

For elephants and rhino, solid, non-expanding bullets are a necessity and many (myself included) preferred them for buffalo also. Hornady steel-jacket "solids" are quite reliable and are used, I believe, in most present-day U.S. factory solid-bullet loads for the .458 and the .375 H & H. Trophy Bonded makes a great flat-nose "solid" that probably chops a wider channel and tends to maintain a straighter course than similar, round-nose bullets. It uses a hardened lead core bonded inside a thick naval bronze jacket. Both Barnes and A-Square make homogenous "solids" from bronze-like alloys. They contain no lead and while less likely to be deformed, they are longer and probably not as well stabilized after impact as the denser and shorter lead-core bullets. Remington uses the Barnes "Super Solid" 400-gr. homogenous, bullet for their .416 Remington Magnum.

I used to advise clients to bring a scope-sighted .375 H & H for dangerous game, or else borrow mine. The reason was that the majority of them were able to place their shots better with it than with an iron-sighted .458 or some other "heavy", and well-placed shots save the professional much trouble and his wife much grief. The .375 was, and is, the legal minimum for dangerous game in several countries and still remains the one outstanding choice for the hunter who wants a rifle that works well on everything from little gazelles to five-ton elephants. My present .375 has done exactly that, in addition to having given quite satisfactory results on the 48 buffalo taken with it — mostly in the hands of various clients. I think a good quality 2½ X scope is about the ideal sight for a .375, and although mine was fitted with iron sights as well, I never used them on game, even when following up wounded buffalo. I depended instead on the Weaver K2.5 steel-tubed scope that was fitted to the rifle when I purchased it.

As the heavy half of a two-gun battery, a scope-sighted .416 might thump the big stuff slightly harder than a .375, if the shooter can handle it equally well. Of those presently offered, I think the .416 Remington Magnum is the best choice for most hunters. Remington rifles and superb Remington factory-loaded ammunition are readily available, and the cartridge matches the ballistics claimed for the legendary .416 Rigby while using a case that will function in standard long magnum actions. Magazine capacity is enhanced by one round compared to the Rigby cartridge. Factory-loaded .416 Remington Magnum ammunition seems to attain the claimed velocity, in fact, all that I have so far chronographed achieved 2,400 fps in my 22-inch barrel. A .416 will shove one back harder than a .375, but still not so horrendously that most hunters could not learn to tolerate it for a few shots on game. Reasonable gun weight will help, as will a thick Pachmayr "Decelerator" recoil pad, and practice sessions should be restricted to five or 10 shots at a time until one becomes accustomed to the rifle. The .416 Remington Magnum has practically as flat a trajectory as the .375 H & H, while providing more energy than the .458 Winchester Magnum at any range — quite a cartridge.

As for African non-dangerous game animals, anything from the 6.5x54 mm Mannlicher-Schoenauer or the 7mm Mauser on up will do just splendidly — as my father and his friends proved beyond quibbling — provided it is pointed right and used with bullets that will give the requisite penetration.

Of the more modern cartridges I think the .243 Winchester should be limited to impala, bushbuck, the gazelles and such deer-size game, and even then there are better choices. I see no sense in taking a .243 or any of the small .25"-calibers to Africa, except for use by a child or a slight woman who simply cannot tolerate any more recoil. We had a .257 Weatherby Magnum on one safari. Used with 117-gr. Nosler Partition bullets its performance on game up to and including zebra was perfect, one-shot kills every time. But the hunter was a fine shot who placed his bullets precisely and, as it happened, none of them encountered really solid bone.

I believe that I have seen a higher proportion of clean one-shot kills made on African plains game (much of it is

81

actually bush-dwelling) with the .270 Winchester than with any other cartridge. The reason, I believe, is that its flat trajectory and mild recoil enable most hunters to place their shots nicely, while its heavier bullet gives sufficient penetration for most purposes. One of the biggest eland we ever collected was taken with a .270. We found a group of six bulls out on a flat, short-grass plain. There was no cover, so the best we could do was to pretend we were a bunch of Masai traveling from one *manyatta* to another. We walked openly and casually obliquely towards them, talking to each other and showing no interest in them at all. And it worked, after a fashion. Eventually, when the range was down to about 300 yards and the bulls were about to join up with a huge herd of cow eland, the biggest bull stopped and turned to stare at us. I told my hunter to lie down, rest his forward hand on an opportune little termite mound and have a go. At the shot the huge beast bucked, ran 20 paces and collapsed more or less in mid-stride. The 150-gr. bullet had removed the top of its heart and I doubt that even the biggest magnum could have done any better.

Anything the .270 Winchester can do, the .280 Remington and the ballistically identical 7x64 mm Brenneke can match, while for the largest antelope their 160- or 175-gr. bullets might be preferable to 150-gr. bullets in the .270.

Bob Bajan used a pre-64 Winchester Model 70, .30-'06 with 180-gr. bullets for all his non-dangerous game on a hunt with me in Kenya. It gave him one-shot kills on everything he fired at, from a 60-pound Thomson's gazelle to impala, *granti*, hartebeest, zebra and a 1,200-pound eland. The .30-'06 works, period.

All these cartridges, and the .308 Winchester, can be sighted to give a point-blank range, out to which the bullet will be within four inches of the line of sight of between 250 and 300 yards. Seldom will a longer shot be called for, but on the rare occasions when it might be justified, the flatter trajectory and long range thump of a magnum would be an advantage. A 7mm magnum (Remington's, Weatherby's or any other, for that matter) with 160-gr. premium bullets makes a superb cartridge for African non-dangerous game out to any responsible range and most hunters can handle it well. The .300 magnums with 180- or 200-gr. bullets ought to be better still, but their recoil is such that, of the hunters I guided who used them, fully a third had some trouble with flinching.

If I had to recommend a two-rifle battery for a general-bag African hunt, I would choose a .416 Remington Magnum fitted with a 2½ X scope for the big stuff (provided, of course, that one can handle its recoil, otherwise, a .375 H & H would be better). For a light rifle I would personally pick a good quality .30-'06 bolt gun fitted with a sturdy, fixed 4 X scope and I would zero it to strike three inches high at 100 yards with 180-gr. premium controlled-expansion bullets. A .270 or .280 would be equally satisfactory, probably, and many might prefer a 7mm magnum. Most hunters these days insist on variable-power scopes, in which case the 2X-7X range should be perfect. African hunting can be hard on rifles, not least the jolting, dust and vibration they may be subjected to in the hunting car, therefore it is well to avoid the gimmicks, and to keep everything as rugged and simple as possible.

Apart from that, the whole secret is to use a bullet that will, *without fail*, give sufficient penetration and to stick it in the right place. Under those circumstances, no game animal in Africa, or anywhere else on earth, will prove to be very tough.

9

Camels And A Leopard

The camel curled its split upper lip and, with a snarling roar, voiced a protest at the cargo it was expected to carry. But Nagwenya just laughed, feinted as if to smack it on the nose, put a foot on the kneeling beast's flank and hauled even harder on the stout rope that he was using to tie down the load.

A few years earlier the Kenya Game Department, in its wisdom, had declared that several hunting blocks would henceforth be "wilderness areas" as far as hunting was concerned. Motor vehicles were not permitted to enter these blocks. Instead one met a game department-owned camel train at a pre-arranged spot on the border of the area, transferred his gear to the baggage animals, mounted a scrubby but awfully hardy Somali pony and set off into the blue at the head of the safari. It was something like a cross between Theodore Roosevelt and Lawrence of Arabia.

Actually, it was a lot of fun and a good way to go. Far too much modern hunting is under pressure, especially as regards time. "Gotta get that record book trophy in the next two days, and move on!" One cannot even begin to understand the soul of

AAGAARD'S AFRICA

Africa by rushing around it in a Toyota. It is necessary to live for a while by the ages-old rhythm imposed by the sun's journey across the sky and by the shifting of the seasons, and to travel at the natural pace of the wilderness. A camel caravan forces the traveler to slow down.

We met the camels at Barsaloi, in Kenya's Northern Frontier District, a harsh, dry land of thorn brush, rock and mirage, where the noonday sky glowed molten white and the sun smote like a sword. It is the country of the Samburu, cattle-herding kin of the Masai, whose long, delicate spears carry leaf-shaped blades; of the wild Boran and of the dark, tough and utterly ruthless Turkana, whom everyone disdains because they will eat anything, even crocodiles.

It is not a gentle place. It tolerates few mistakes and encourages no illusions. If one screws up, the chances are he will die. The tribes still raid each other for livestock and women — and for the joy of killing. Death is commonplace, life is short and fleeting, and is lived intensely. There are few places where one can get back so close to the realities of life as in this elemental land and that, in large measure, is its fascination.

The country is cut up by *luggas*, dry rivers that run down from the Karisia Hills and wind across the flatter country until they join the great Milgis Lugga. They can be dangerous at times, because a thunderstorm miles up in the hills can bring down a sudden, roaring, bank-to-bank flood with virtually no warning. But most of the year they are dry and, as their wide, sandy beds provide easy going, they form the natural highways in that region.

There is no surface water except during the rains. Water is obtained by digging in the right spot in the bed of a *lugga*. Where to dig is a matter of experience. Elephants seem to have the gift and, as they are surprisingly good at digging, they create many of the waterholes. Life revolves around the availability of water. Camels may be able to go a week without a drink, depending on conditions, but cattle, horses and men cannot. A knowledge of the location and state of the waterholes is an essential prerequisite to non-motorized travel in that country.

The safari left the road about mid-morning and set off up the Barsaloi Lugga towards the hills. ("Road" may be a pretentious description for two dusty ruts. I doubt that a hundred vehicles a year passed that way.) Apart from Joe Cheffings and myself, our clients, Doctors Joey Pirung and Herb Buetel from Mesquite, Texas, and our regular trackers, cook and camp staff, we had a dozen government pack camels tied head to tail in strings of four, with each string led by a cameleer on foot.

And far from least, we had Nagwenya, a Ndorobo tribesman from Dol Dol. As neither Joe nor I had been in this particular area before, we had consulted with Julian McKeand, a professional hunter who specialized in the Northern Frontier District. He very kindly sent Nagwenya, one of his best trackers, to help us. The Ndorobo are a mixed and scattered tribe of outcasts, hunters and traders with a reputation for living by their wits. Nagwenya not only knew the country well, but understood the management of camels and could speak all the local languages. He was an invaluable rogue, and a cheerful, amusing and thoroughly likable companion to boot.

Our destination was a waterhole about six hours' march in from the road. Here several tributary *luggas* and ravines ran into the Barsaloi and the area was said to contain an extraordinary concentration of leopards. We plodded along the glaring white sand, with the wooden camel bells clonking monotonously behind us. Joe and our two Texans bestrode the Somali ponies with their feet almost dragging on the ground, but I preferred to walk. A fleeting thunderstorm the previous night had left a few ephemeral puddles of water on the sand, but they would be gone before sundown. At long last we came to the waterhole and set up camp on some flat ground safely above the bed of the *lugga*, in a grove of fair-sized acacia trees.

While we put up tents for the clients, every one else slept under the stars. But we had a tiny refrigerator that ran on bottled gas, good camp cots, Coleman-type lamps, a folding table and chairs, and a canvas bucket with a shower head hung from a convenient branch — what more could one desire? Pretty soon Nzioka had supper ready, and afterwards it was cool enough to sit by a campfire, clean, full and relaxed, with a drink in hand and the talk going slow and easy.

The next morning we buckled down to the serious business of hunting leopard. The only practical way to catch a leopard is to bait it. Whether one could be brought to bay with hounds I do not know. I have never heard of anyone trying it and, in any case, it would have been illegal.

Leopards like to stash their own kills up in trees, presumably to keep them safe from hyenas, lions and other scavengers. They apparently have no compunction about stealing another's kill, though, and will happily appropriate meat they find hanging in a suitable tree without seeming to wonder how it got there. But, the leopard hunter cannot hang his bait in any old tree. It has to be in an area that leopards use, near a route they are likely to travel. It has to be a tree that a leopard would like to find a meal in and one situated so that a leopard will feel secure enough about it to visit while there is still daylight. (I hear that, nowadays, they shoot leopards at night with the aid of a spotlight and call it sport. When I was guiding, anyone who did that would have been thrown in jail and rightly so.)

The first order of business was to find suitable trees and get some baits hung. In the old days, baits were no problem. There were enough animals allowed on the license that one could shoot as many as he needed, and warthogs and such were regarded as vermin. This was no longer the case and some forethought as to what to use was now required. We had brought with us most of the four quarters of a Grevy's zebra Herb had killed a couple of days previously and that gave us something to start.

Joe and Joey went one way, Herb and I another. Each party had a tracker, a *syce* to hold the horses, a pack camel on which to

A HUNTER REMEMBERS

bring in any game bagged and a camelman — quite a cavalcade. One morning I dropped out to take care of some business — behind a bush. When I caught up with the party again, I was startled to see a zebra tagging along behind the camel. The zebra suddenly stopped, looked about as if in astonished horror, then wheeled around and was gone with a frantic clatter of hooves. It had finally realized that the thing it was following really bore no resemblance to anyone it knew.

We each put up three or four baits. Herb shot quite a nice impala one day, most of which we also used for bait, and a good gerenuk (giraffe-necked gazelle) which we saved for camp meat. Joe and Joey hung one bait not a hundred yards from camp, in a tree where Nagwenya said they had had leopards feeding before. Then it was a matter of checking the baits.

The first one to be hit was the camp tree. Something had taken a good feed from it, there were fresh claw marks on the trunk of the tree, and big tracks in the *lugga* nearby. Joe already had the blind built, now he checked it over, replenished grass and leaves where necessary, put up a tripod just the right height to support Joey's .300 Weatherby Magnum from the sitting position, made sure he had a clear view of the bait and the limb on which the leopard would have to stand to feed, and swept the ground inside free of dry leaves, twigs and clinking pebbles.

Herb and I had got back quite early that evening, so we were in camp at about four in the afternoon, when Joey and Joe crawled into their blind. Everyone made an effort to be quiet, but there was still a muted murmur of voices, the occasional clang of a cooking pot. Herb and I took showers, drank tea and waited, pretending to read some old, and well worn, magazines.

It came at about 5:30 p.m., the shockingly sudden crack of the Weatherby. In the moment of stillness as the echoes faded away, I clearly heard the rattle of the bolt as Joey reloaded. The whole camp froze, listening intently. Then there was a loud shout in jubilation from the blind.

"We got him," came the shout of triumph. "WE GOT HIM!"

89

AAGAARD'S AFRICA

The leopard had materialized out of nothing. One moment the tree was empty, the next the big cat was standing on the feeding limb, looking around arrogantly and twitching the end of its tail. Joe waited until it had started to feed, then he nudged Joey, pointed with his chin and silently mouthed the order, "Shoot him. Now!"

Joey shot and the leopard fell out of the tree with all four feet uppermost. The nicest sound of all in leopard hunting is the solid thump like a sack of meal when one hits the ground stone dead and the hunter knows he isn't going to have to crawl around in the shrubbery to find it. Joey's *chui* landed thus and why not? If there is a more viciously effective leopard cartridge than the .300 Weatherby with a 150-gr. bullet, I cannot imagine what it might be. The hunter still has to stick the bullet into the right place, though, and Joey had done exactly that.

The next morning we found that another bait a mile or so down the *lugga* had been fed on and built a blind by it. Ideally, the blind should be built when the bait is hung, so that the leopard will not spot any suspicious changes in the environs after it has started patronizing the tree. But there is a lot of work in a proper blind, so we sometimes took a chance by not making one until we had a customer.

The purpose of the blind is to conceal the hunters. The wall facing the bait must be thick enough to preclude the leopard from being able to spot any movement within and the blind ought to be roofed over to provide black, all-concealing shade inside. The shooting hole is no larger than necessary and is normally plugged with a wad of grass until the hunters are settled into position, because the unpredictable cat may already be up the tree when they arrive on the scene. For the same reason, the blind should be situated so that one can approach and enter it without being seen from the tree. Compared to many other wild animals, leopards (and lions) do not seem to have a well-developed sense of smell, which may be why they often do not find a bait until it is quite "ripe". I have known

90

leopards to come to a bait that was directly downwind from an occupied blind, nevertheless it is well to give some consideration to the prevailing breeze when deciding where to build a blind.

We made a circular blind from brush cut some distance away and situated it on the edge of a gully about 50 yards from the tree. It was just big enough to hold three of us comfortably and had an entrance on the opposite side from the bait tree.

We sneaked into it about mid-afternoon, Herb, Kinuno the tracker and I, and settled down to wait. Beside the shooting port there was a small peep hole where Kinuno stationed himself to watch, while Herb and I kept our heads down and read a paperback book apiece. The theory was that the leopard would be far less likely to spot Kinuno's dark face than Herb's or my pale ones.

It was a hot afternoon. The flies buzzed around, ants crawled over us, and time passed slowly until a startled spurfowl flew up onto a branch and began squawking its alarm at something down below. Kinuno looked around at us, grinned tightly and pointed towards the bird. We waited in tense expectation while Kinuno kept his gaze rivetted to the bait tree. But nothing happened and presently the spurfowl flew down and went about its business. It seemed a false alarm, so we started to relax.

Then I happened to glance behind me out of the entrance and there was a leopard 20 yards across the little draw, staring into the blind with an expression of bemused interest, as if it had never seen anything half so curious in its life before. But as I reached out to grab Herb's arm and draw his attention to this phenomenon, the leopard turned and streaked away. That was it. That particular bait was not touched again. We should, of course, have closed the entrance after we had crawled into the blind, but for some reason we had failed to do so.

The same evening Joey took his movie camera and sat in the blind by the camp where he had shot his leopard the previous afternoon. Incredibly, a big female leopard with a cub appeared; and well before dark so that photographing them was feasible.

AAGAARD'S AFRICA

They fed on the remnants of the kill, licked and groomed each other and put on quite a show for the camera.

A couple of days later another bait not half a mile from camp was hit. It was in a big acacia growing on a bluff overlooking the *lugga*. The bait was suspended so that a leopard could reach it only along one long, horizontal branch, where it would be clearly delineated against the sky. The trunk and the limb were all scratched up with old clawmarks. Nagwenya plucked a black and white hair from the bark and smiled confidently.

"No leopard has ever fed in this tree and lived to tell the tale," he said.

Perhaps so, but it seemed that this one might be the exception. We refurbished the old blind and waited in it that afternoon. Just before sunset there was a rumble of hooves on rock and a tumult of bells, lowing kine and sharp shouts as a Samburu stripling drove his herd homeward, passing right under the bait tree. We stayed until full dark, but nothing came.

We tried again the next evening. This time there was no disturbance, but again we saw nothing. However, the bait was being fed on every night, so it was obvious that the leopard was coming after nightfall.

We decided that we would have to try to sneak into the blind in the dark before dawn and see whether we might catch old *chui* still lingering in the tree at first light. The trick would be to reach the blind without the leopard becoming aware of us. We cut steps up the side of the bluff behind the blind, cleared a track we could crawl along to the entrance, practiced the whole maneuver several times and then flagged the route with strips of tissue paper to enable us to follow it by starlight. We were careful to ensure that the sling swivels on our rifles could not squeak or rattle and that there was nothing in our pockets to clink. We removed our watches, as it has been suggested that a leopard may be able to hear the ticking, or even more so the high pitched hum from some of the newfangled electronic ones.

I thought we had got into the blind very quietly, no one had tripped, kicked a stone, or coughed. So it was a disappointment when Kinuno peered through the peephole as soon as it was light enough to see and then shrugged to indicate that there was nothing. I took a look. I could just discern the bait, but the feeding branch was empty. Then as I watched something stirred in the dark shadow in the fork of the tree, and a leopard flowed up onto the branch and walked out along it.

It can be difficult to determine the sex of a leopard with certainty under these circumstances. Females were legal, but we by all means avoided shooting them. This one had a heavy neck and a muscular, indefinably masculine look about it, so I waited until it had started tearing at the kill, then nodded at Herb and motioned for him to shoot.

Herb was using a Belgian-made Browning Safari bolt-action 7mm Remington Magnum, with which he shot very nicely. The 150-gr. bullet plucked the leopard from the branch as suddenly as you please and flung it to the ground where it managed only a couple of faint growls before all was quiet.

We left Herb in solitude to contemplate his leopard while we went to camp for a camel and an elated throng came back with us to escort the prize home.

Next morning as the safari headed out towards Barsaloi there were fresh elephant tracks in the *lugga*, moist, aromatic, ball-shaped droppings littered the sand and a new waterhole had been dug in a bend under a high bank.

When we reached the road and our vehicles, Nagwenya tugged on a camel's lead-rope.

"Hup!" he ordered, and the beast obediently knelt down with a rocking motion, first one end, then the other. But as he started to unload it, it swung its head round at him, spitting and snarling in furious protest. Camels are something else again.

10

Elephant Hunting, As It Used To Be

Men, who were hunting elephants long before the present species appeared on the scene, are the only predators that the African elephant has ever had to fear. Lions may take an occasional calf — though rarely, for elephant mothers firmly believe in stamping out any threats to their young — but cannot do much with adults weighing from three to over six tons.

Exactly when man began hunting elephants is unclear. The remains of an obvious butchering site in Tanzania's Olduvai Gorge, where stone cutting tools and points are intermingled with fossilized elephant bones, have been dated to well over one million years ago, so we were quite likely already at it by then. It had to have been a terrifyingly dangerous business, even when the great beasts were driven into a swamp and mired down before being attacked with rocks and stone-tipped spears. But the reward, in the form of several thousand pounds of food, must have seemed worth the risk of losing an occasional hunter.

AAGAARD'S AFRICA

One must wonder how prehistoric man utilized and preserved the meat? No doubt an entire tribe would camp by the carcass and feast mightily. Then they probably cut the flesh into thin strips and hung it on trees and bushes to dry in the sun and form jerky (or *biltong*), just as most modern Africans do with the flesh of hunted animals that they wish to preserve.

Among those who have and who probably continue to hunt the elephant are the Waliangulu, a small and mysterious tribe the existence of which was largely unknown to the outside world until the vast and seemingly unpopulated Tsavo country was proclaimed a national park in 1948.

"Where No Vultures Fly" had been the slogan (and the name of a movie) in the campaign to get national parks established in East Africa, but the first park wardens into Tsavo were horrified to find dark clouds of vultures swarming over large sections of the park and dead elephants everywhere. The elephants, to the astonishment of officials, had been killed by arrows.

Then it was learned that, since time out of mind, the Waliangulu (also known as the Waata) had been using the long bow and poisoned arrows to hunt the elephants of Tsavo. The Waliangulu's poison, a type used by many different tribes, is made by boiling the wood and bark of the Acokanthera tree until a black, tar-like mess is left. A thick layer of the substance is smeared on the arrow just behind the head, and a strip of soft leather (often dik-dik hide) is wound over it to protect it from dampness and sunlight, both of which hasten its deterioration. Though there is no known antidote for this poison, it has to be introduced into the bloodstream in order to work and, because it is broken down by the digestive processes, the meat from animals killed by it can be eaten with no ill effects.

When the poison is fresh and potent, death usually comes within a few minutes after the quarry is struck. But if the poison is old and deteriorated it may take several days to kill, or it may fail to do so entirely. I have found poisoned arrow heads in a zebra and an eland, both of which were in perfect health when I

96

A HUNTER REMEMBERS

shot them. The iron arrowheads were encapsulated in a black, gristly material and the wounds had healed so that hardly a trace of them was evident on the hides.

As they rely on the poison to do the work, the bows of most Kenya tribes are comparatively light affairs about four feet long and generally pull less than 50 pounds. In contrast, the bows of the Waliangulu elephant hunters, who seldom bothered much with lesser game, were up to six feet in length and almost as thick as a man's wrist through the grip. They pulled from 100 to 130 pounds and the bowstrings were of twisted sinew. The technique used in drawing the bow was to raise it high, then jerk it down, pushing it powerfully away with one hand while pulling the string back with three fingers of the other. Its wielders could be recognized by the distinctive musculature they developed.

The arrows were often made in three sections. The main shaft, fletched (unusually) with four vanes of vulture feathers, had a rawhide-bound socket into which the poison-bearing fore-shaft fitted. It, in turn, carried the iron broadhead. The whole missile was some three feet long, but after delivering its payload the main shaft was designed to bounce off the animal's hide so that it could be picked up and used again.

The Waliangulu bow was a formidable weapon indeed, but its devotees were equally redoubtable — superb hunters whose bushcraft, tracking skills, knowledge of the game, hardiness and audacity are virtually unsurpassed.

As among all hunters, primitive or modern, elephant hunters disagree as to the best spot to aim for. The chest shot was avoided, because even with so powerful a bow, getting a soft iron arrowhead through the rib cage was problematical. Some experts liked to go for the spleen or the kidneys, while the majority seemed to believe that the liver shot was the more deadly. It was, in any case, necessary to get close, ten paces being considered a proper sort of range. Consequently, the hunter would often be in the middle of the ensuing pandemonium, with terrified, screaming elephants rushing about in all directions. No doubt it served to keep a hunter alert and quick on his feet.

Originally when a Waliangulu killed an elephant, his whole family would camp by it until they had consumed it. But in later times they killed many more elephants and rhinos than they needed for food, in order to sell the tusks or horns to dealers in illegal ivory. A loud and emotional outcry was raised against these terrible "poachers", and strenuous efforts were made to eliminate their way of life. They were hunted down, prosecuted and jailed, though with what justice is questionable. It always seemed to me that the Waliangulu, who went eyeball to eyeball with the elephants they poached (or hunted, as the case may be) had a certain claim to the Tsavo elephants (certainly a better claim than the heavily-armed, poaching gangs of today), and I've never been able to suppress a certain sympathy and admiration for them.

Elephants have been taken in pit traps, encircled by fire, caught in snares, killed by weighed spears suspended over their trails and hamstrung by the Arab sword-hunters of the Atbara region of the Sudan.

These latter chaps and their hunting methods are described by Sir Samuel Baker in his *The Nile Tributaries of Abyssinia*, first published in 1874. Baker, who traveled through Abyssinia in 1861, described these hunters and their weapon, which resembled a crusader's sword, with a straight, double-edged blade about 36 inches in length and a hilt with cross-bar quillons. For hunting, the first nine inches of the blade was bound with cord, so that the sword could be swung two-handed and the rest was stropped to razor-keen sharpness.

A party of three or four of these swordsmen would ride out together and find a lone bull elephant, or separate one from its companions. They would then provoke a charge and one of the party would flee just ahead of the elephant, so as to engage its full attention, while the others closed in from behind. At an

A HUNTER REMEMBERS

opportune moment one of the latter would leap from his galloping horse with drawn sword and endeavor to cut the elephant's Achilles tendon with one slash of his blade.

If he succeeded, the beast was immediately immobilized, for an elephant cannot travel on three legs. The lead man would then turn and taunt the elephant into attempting another charge, giving the swordsman an excellent chance to slash the tendon of the other leg. With the arteries of both legs cut as well, the elephant would quickly bleed to death.

That, at least, is how it was supposed to go. But if the decoy's horse stumbled on a rock or hole while galloping over the rough ground, or if the swordsman missed his stroke in the slightest, the outcome might be smashingly different.

Sir Samuel, who had killed wild boar and sambar (an Asiatic relative of the European red deer) with the dagger and was thus no stranger to close quarters, remarked, "This extraordinary hunting is attended with superlative danger, and the hunters frequently fall victims to their intrepidity. I felt inclined to take off my cap and make a low bow to the gallant and swarthy fellows who sat before me, when I knew the toughness of their hearts and the activity of their limbs."

Although cruel by our standards, this is probably as sporting a method of hunting elephants as has ever been devised. However, Rennie Bere, a former Chief Warden of the Uganda National Parks, has related an even more astonishing act of individual gallantry.

During a drought in the Acholi country, a big bull elephant took possession of the only waterhole for miles around, killed two women and prevented anyone from drawing water. After several rifle-armed hunters had failed to deal with it because it retired into thick cover whenever they tried to approach, Edward Omara, a tribesman whom Bere described as the bravest of the old-time hunters, went to the waterhole alone. There he provoked a charge, stood his ground and killed the marauding elephant, singlehandedly, using only his spear.

AAGAARD'S AFRICA

As anyone who has faced a charging elephant knows, that took an incredible amount of intestinal fortitude. But one is also left wondering, how did he do it? An Acholi spearhead of untempered iron would hardly have sufficient penetration to reach the brain from in front, so possibly he slammed it into the base of the throat, where it would have a chance of penetrating sufficiently far to reach the heart or some of the great blood vessels — maybe. Or perhaps he was able to dodge aside at the last moment and then drive the spear in close behind the bull's shoulder as it swept past him. In any event, he would have had to let it get awfully close and, as a spear does not have the power to stop an angry elephant in its tracks, some very nimble evasive action must have been required on his part. For his bravery Omara was awarded a well-deserved George Cross, a civilian award for valor equal to the British soldier's Victoria Cross, or our Medal of Honor.

Sir Samuel Baker, who finished his career as an Egyptian *pasha* governing the Equatoria Province of the Sudan for the Khedive of Egypt, was himself a remarkable man. He was a hunter, military commander, administrator, explorer and Fellow of the Royal Geographic Society, the author of several books and an authority on sporting firearms. He hunted all over Ceylon and India, in parts of Africa and even in the American West. He spent the years 1861-1865 exploring the Nile tributaries and tracing the White Nile to Lake Albert, which he named. Though the country was in a condition of total anarchy due to the raids of slave traders from Khartoum, he was accompanied through-out by his beautiful young wife, Florence, who, he said, was not the type to scream.

As mentioned, Baker regularly killed wild boar and deer with a hunting knife, first bringing them to bay with his hounds. But one incident with a water buffalo was out of the ordinary and is worth recounting.

Baker was hunting on the plain of Minneria in Ceylon (now Sri Lanka) with a companion who shot a water buffalo using a muzzle-loading rifle that was too light for the job at hand, even though it was of 20-bore and carried a double charge of powder. The animal fell at the shot and lay still until Baker and his companion reached it. Then, in Sir Samuel's words, "The apparently dead buffalo sprang to its feet and blundered straight at [my astonished companion] who was not three feet distant. He attempted to jump backward, but...tripped, and fell flat upon his back, immediately in the path of the savage bull. Instinctively, as quick as lightning, my right hand had drawn my long hunting knife and plunged it hilt-deep exactly behind the shoulder. To my amazement the buffalo fell to the blow and...this time the mighty bull was beyond recovery.... The knife was a portion of a real old 'Andrea Ferrara' Highland claymore. The blade was 18 inches in length and two inches in breadth, double-edged, and as sharp as it was possible to make it."

All the same, Baker rather preferred to use a double-barrel, eight-bore, muzzle-loading rifle on water buffalo and Indian elephants. Or, better yet, a single-barrel "three-ounce" rifle (meaning it threw a ball of that weight) by Gibbs of Bristol. It had a 36-inch barrel and weighed 21 pounds. Of it, he wrote, "The three-ounce was an absolute exterminator, and no buffalo had a chance..."

Even more impressive was his "Baby", a single barrel rifle by Holland that carried a half-pound shell with a bursting charge of half-an-ounce of fine powder. The awed Arabs called it "*Junna el Mootfah*", the child of a cannon. One might be excused for imagining that this precocious infant would summarily upend even the greatest bull elephant under any circumstances, but it did not do so.

In the Sudan, Baker used "Baby" to shoot a very large cow elephant that was turned obliquely away from him. The explosive shell entered the right flank, breaking a rib on which it exploded, then passed through the stomach and the lower portions of both lungs, which were severely damaged, before coming to rest beneath the skin of the opposite shoulder. Sir

AAGAARD'S AFRICA

Samuel recorded that the recoil of "Baby", loaded with 10 drachms (approximately 273.4 grains) of the strongest powder, spun him around like a top.

"It was difficult," he reported, "to say which was staggered the most severely, the elephant or myself...."

The cow traveled 300 yards before falling and was not found until the next day.

On another hunt a bull elephant took the half-pound shell "directly behind the shoulder". This elephant, too, failed to drop to the shot, but ran 150 yards, which is what one could expect with similar placement when using a mild little smallbore like the .458 Winchester Magnum.

On that occasion "Baby" again spun Baker around like a weathercock and, as it recoiled, drove its hammer deep into the bridge of his nose. So it is perhaps not surprising that he subsequently settled on four double-barrel 10-ga. rifles as constituting the ideal battery for elephant hunting. He preferred to use a round ball, hardened in the proportion of 1:12 with mercury (a dangerous procedure) and propelled by seven drachms (191.4 grains) of blackpowder.

In Ceylon, when so armed, he had been wont to wait until a charging elephant was almost upon him before flooring it with a frontal brain shot. To his dismay he found that the tactic was not reliable on African elephants, not even on cows.

Once, when a cow elephant came for him, Baker waited coolly until she was within four paces before giving her a 10-ga. ball in exactly the right spot on the forehead. Its only effect was to make the cow stagger back a step or two before coming on again. The contents of Baker's second barrel checked the cow and caused her to back off into a thicket, trumpeting with rage. Sir Samuel snatched another 10-ga. from a gunbearer, ran straight in at the elephant and gave it a third, carefully aimed, shot to the head, the result of which was a decisive charge. I imagine that even the doughty Sir Samuel was becoming a little perturbed at this point, but luckily one of the swordhunters was able to dash in and immobilize the elephant with a slash to the hind leg. Baker found that his three shots, which struck within a three-inch group, had all been properly placed. The 10-ga. rifle simply lacked the penetration to reach the brain from in front, though it was deadly on a side brain shot.

By most accounts from this period, it seems that blackpowder elephant guns with their lead bullets were generally deficient in penetration, particularly for frontal brain shots. Thus, throughout the blackpowder era hunters lacked the means of stopping a charging African elephant with any certainty.

Frederick Courtenay Selous, who at age 65 was killed in action against the Germans in what is now Tanzania and whose grave lies in the great Selous Game Reserve in that country, was among the most famous of all the African hunters, largely because he wrote so well about it.

He started his elephant hunting career in South Africa using a pair of smoothbore 4-ga. muzzle-loaders, which were reloaded on the run by just dipping a handful of blackpowder from a leather bag slung at one's side. Selous was a commercial ivory hunter, often working with a partner or two. When they got into a herd they would shoot quickly in an endeavor to secure as many jumbos as possible while they had the opportunity.

On one such occasion Selous's gun misfired. Hurriedly, he threw it back to his gunbearer in exchange for a freshly loaded one. Amidst the horrendous thundering of the four-bores, the rolling clouds of white smoke and the terrified screaming of the elephants, the gunbearer thought the piece had been discharged. He threw another handful of powder down the barrel, rammed a four-ounce ball on top of it and placed a fresh cap on the nipple. A short while later Selous was presented with a shot at the shoulder of a big bull. He was carrying the unknowingly double-charged rifle and this time it fired. The recoil lifted Selous off his feet and threw him to the ground. The gun itself came to earth several yards away, its stock shattered.

The elephant stopped, but did not fall. Selous approached to within 40 yards and sat down to fire his second rifle, only to find that he could not raise his right arm. He had to have his gunbearer massage it for several minutes before he was able to shoot the elephant again, carefully. On receiving the ball from Selous's second rifle, the bull walked quickly away. Selous ran after it for upwards of a mile, but still being somewhat shaken, he was unable to close with it, so sent his gunbearer ahead to turn it. The upshot was that the bull came directly at Selous. Its trunk hung straight down shielding its chest, leaving him no option but to try for the brain.

Selous wrote, "...the imminence of danger braced up my nerves and I think that I never held a gun steadier than upon this occasion." Immediately upon firing he dodged out to the side, but when he glanced back he saw the elephant standing with blood running down from a wound between its eyes, exactly at the point of Selous's aim. Then the bull moved off and it was never recovered despite having absorbed four, 4-ounce balls and something on the order of 10 tons of energy.

Altogether, one is left with the distinct impression that no matter how cavernous their bores, the blackpowder guns with their lead balls left something to be desired as elephant guns. It is no wonder that they were quickly discarded when smokeless powder and jacketed bullets came into use because, when used with round-nose, full-metal-jacket "solid" bullets of good sectional density, even a smallbore like the 6.5mm could reliably reach the brain of the biggest elephant, almost without regard to the angle.

On the other hand, though their guns may have been inadequate, the old-time elephant hunters who used them certainly were not. They were about as tough, deadly and resolute a group of men as have ever lived.

11

Africa's Elephant

The African elephant, *Loxodonta africana*, is the greatest game animal of them all. Africa's old-time professional hunters judged each other largely by the ivory they brought in and big ivory is the most prestigious trophy there is. A great pair of tusks will immediately become the focus and pride of any trophy room, where they will outrank the grand slam of sheep, the tremendous seven-point elk, the beautiful kudu, the assorted bears, leopards, lions and tigers, the bongo, the argali and even a Boone & Crockett whitetail deer rack.

The primary reason for this esteem is the sheer, awful size of the beast, the largest animal that can be taken with a rifle. Even now, after nearly 15 years away from our common home ground, I am still shocked to remember how truly colossal a bull elephant is when one approaches it on foot and looks up at it from a distance of 10 or 12 yards or so. It seems eternal and quite impregnable and one cannot imagine that the puny little .458 rifle the hunter grasps so tightly will do more than merely annoy the monster.

In truth, elephants *are* large. I have never weighed one, needless to say, but the authorities seem to agree that a mature bull will weigh five to seven tons and that a cow will reach upwards of three. An average mature bull stands nine to 10 feet tall at the shoulder, while a maximum height of 13 feet has been alleged. In contrast black rhino and hippo seldom exceed a ton-and-a-half or two tons and most African buffalo bulls probably go under 1,500 pounds, live weight. The biggest Alaskan brown bears may go up to 1,600 pounds, it is said, though the majority of those taken by sportsmen are closer to half that weight. The average Alaskan bull moose probably runs about 1,200 pounds, while adult bull elk usually weigh around 700 to 800 pounds and rarely exceed 1,000 pounds.

The would-be elk hunter who lies awake at night agonizing whether his trusty '06 will do for the bull of his dreams might reflect that, in proportion, it will slam the mightiest elk about six times as hard as a standard elephant gun like the .470 Nitro Express can hit a middling-size jumbo. Even the fearsome .460 Weatherby Magnum strikes a bull elephant with only about 0.7 foot-pounds of energy per pound of the beast's live weight, the equivalent of using the high velocity .22 Long Rifle on a 200-pound whitetail deer. This is no doubt what W.D.M. "Karamoja" Bell had in mind when he said he did not see how anyone could hope to kill an elephant by "shock" unless he hit it with a field gun.

But beside their size, there are many other fascinating things about elephant, not least of which are their teeth. We generally call them "tusks". Tusks are modified incisors (front teeth), not canines as one might imagine. Tusks continue to grow throughout an animal's life, though more slowly as it ages. A tusk weighing 100 pounds will gain the nimrod who collects it the immortal prestige of inclusion in Rowland Ward's famous *Records Of Big Game*, but when I was acting as a professional hunter, ivory that weighed 60 pounds a side was considered very decent.

Elephants use their tusks to dig in the ground for roots or water, to pry bark off trees, occasionally to jab other elephants and to hang their trunks on when they rest. They have also been known to stick them through careless elephant hunters. A good proportion of elephant tusks have had their tips broken at one time or another, though it may not be very noticeable as use tends to sharpen them again. And one tusk of a pair commonly shows more wear than the other, as if its owner had been right- or left-tusked.

Besides the tusks, elephants grow six sets of molar teeth that appear in succession. As one lot is worn out it is replaced by the next set, until all six of them have been used up. Very roughly, depending on the sort of vegetation upon which the animal feeds, each set is good for 10 or 12 years, which gives elephants a maximum life span of around 60 to 70 years.

A bull elephant's enormous ears — shaped rather like a map of Africa — may measure as much as five feet across. They not only assist the animal's acute hearing (acute, that is, when the animal is on the alert and not making too much noise itself), but also act as rather efficient radiators. When a jumbo stands in the shade of a tree, slowly flapping its ears in the noonday heat, the blood leaving its ears may be as much as 16 degrees cooler than the blood entering them.

The most wonderful of the elephant's evolutionary adaptations, however, is its seven-foot long trunk, a writhing mass of tiny muscles that can break off a six-inch thick branch as easily as snapping a twig, pull up a tussock of grass and daintily knock the dirt off it before stuffing it into the beast's mouth, fling a pesky hunter 20 feet up into a thorn tree, or delicately pluck a single fruit or leaf. The elephant uses its trunk to rub its eye, greet a friend or caress a lover, or perhaps to chastise a calf. It drinks by first sucking a gallon or two of water into its trunk and then squirting it down its throat. Dust or mud is also sucked up with the trunk and then blown over the elephant's body. Consequently, like rhino and warthogs, elephants in any particular district tend to be the same color as the termite mounds.

In addition, the trunk remains a nose through which the animal breathes and smells. Elephants have an excellent sense of smell and one must pay the closest attention to the wind when approaching them, or else suddenly all their trunks will go up like periscopes and that will be the end of that stalk. Thus a little porous bag of fine ashes that when shaken will reveal the slightest movement of the air is an essential piece of elephant hunting equipment.

Elephant society is matriarchal, with the basic unit being a family group consisting of a dozen or so related cows and their offspring, led by a tough old biddy who does not stand for much nonsense. Males are driven out of these groups as teenagers, or perhaps just leave on their own accord when they have had enough of domineering females. From then on they live and travel with other bulls or, more rarely, alone joining the cows only sporadically when one may be in heat.

Elephants are extraordinarily complex animals. Scientist Ian Douglas-Hamilton, who spent many years studying them, used to tell of a young adult bull that returned to its family group from time to time for no other apparent reason than to spend a few days with its sister, which was not in *oestrus*. We might reflect on the fact that no ram, bear, moose, kudu or whitetail buck is even aware that it has a sister.

In his book *Elephant*, Royal Navy Commander David Enderby Blunt, who was an elephant control officer in Tanganyika before World War II, describes how he once tried to brain-shoot a crop-raiding bull — with a .303 Lee Enfield — but only succeeded in stunning it. The bull went down and, immediately, "...three others closed in on him, one on either side and one behind, and they just boosted him to his feet and...supporting him on either side set off, wheeling gradually around to the left and back to the forest."

So many other reliable witnesses, including Selous, have reported similar instances that there can be no doubt that elephants will indeed sometimes try to raise a wounded comrade to its feet and help it get away, even at considerable risk to their own lives.

Cow elephants are good mothers and the whole family group

is usually very tolerant of, and protective toward, all the infants. It is not unknown for an abandoned or orphaned calf to be adopted and nursed by another cow, something that is practically unheard of among other animals.

Sometimes elephants will congregate in very large numbers — several hundred cows, calves, young bulls and grand old tuskers all in one huge herd — and there seems to be some excitement in the air on these occasions. After a few days they break up and each group goes its own way. But, what the conclave was about, no human seems ever to know. We got involved with such a gathering once when the buffalo tracks we were following led us into a valley occupied by perhaps 200 jumbos. We would try to work our way carefully around one group, only to have another bunch get our scent. Pretty soon there were mobs of panic-stricken elephants stampeding every which way and altogether it became somewhat hectic.

In contrast to its hearing and sense of smell, an elephant's eyesight is mediocre. When they are not suspicious it is quite easy to get right up to elephants using only the skimpiest cover, or none at all if one moves slowly. On the other hand a bull once saw us moving among trees and brush from a distance of 70 long paces and immediately initiated a dead-serious charge.

Alec Pringle, Kinuno and I had been working this bunch of half-dozen bulls for a couple of hours, trying to get a shot at the biggest, a 70-pounder. The fitful breeze had been shifty in the extreme and the herd had caught a faint swirl of our scent several times. They were alert, suspicious and no doubt exasperated when the second-biggest bull finally spotted us. The wind at that moment was in our favor, so it came by sight. That being the case it seemed unlikely that we could evade it by running aside and, anyway, its ivory appeared satisfactory, so I called to Alec, "Shoot!" At that moment the elephant's head disappeared behind the leafy branches of a nearby tree and we had to wait until it cleared it. Then, when I raised the .458, I could not see the sights. The leaf of the Mauser safety was still in the upright, half-on position. In those days my thumb automatically flicked the safety off as the rifle came up without my having to think about it, but this time the reflex failed me.

I blessed old Paul Mauser then, for with any other safety catch I might have pulled and pulled and pulled, wondering why the blasted gun would not fire, until the beast trundled over me. I put matters right, but Alec beat me to the shot using my old .375 with its Weaver K2.5 scope and the elephant was already dropping as I fired. It went down on its knees and forthwith started to get up. Alec and I hammered it in unison, then poured in a couple more for safety's sake. The bull's forehead lay 14 paces from where we had stood. Later we recovered one of Alec's bullets, a Hornady 300-gr. steel-jacket "solid" from a handload a previous client had given me, from close behind the base of one of the jumbo's ears. It was so completely undeformed that it could have been used again, but after penetrating the brain it had veered almost a foot off course.

The whole safari crew wagered as to the weight of the tusks. I made it a rule to always give clients a conservative estimate, so I guessed them at 45 pounds apiece, hoping they would go 50 pounds. But when Berit and Alec's wife, Gail, who were in camp with us (together with the Pringle's five-month-old son Todd), took the tusks to the closest railway station, the freight scales recorded them at 60½ and 61½ pounds respectively and Nzioka, our camp's cook, won the jackpot.

Actually, determined attacks by unwounded elephants are not common and most charges are only demonstrations meant to frighten an intruder away. When an elephant shuffles its feet, shakes its head and makes a lot of noise while backing and filling before coming on, it is usually bluffing. When it means business an elephant launches its charge with little warning, and comes silently and with deadly determination. At least I believe it comes silently, but I could be wrong.

The first time I stood an elephant's charge, the people with me were impressed by how loudly the cow trumpeted as she came. My own recollection is that, when she came, she came without a sound.

It was a matriarch who was demonstrating to cover the retreat of its family, which is what most "charges" from cows are about. Not all of them are bluffs, however. Johnny Uys, a very experienced professional hunter, was killed by a cow elephant in the Kafue National Park in Zambia. From what I hear, he was armed and was covering the retreat of his party of tourists from a belligerent cow. In an attempt to stop the harridan without killing it he put a shot through its ear, which usually does the trick, but it came on and got to him before he could fire again.

Despite Alec Pringle's and my little adventure, the really big tuskers seldom charge. They have learned that discretion is expedient if they wish to retain their ivory for themselves, and usually prefer to fade away and leave for a distant destination at the first hint of trouble.

Following up a wounded bull is another matter. Then, a charge is to be expected. A close quarter attack can also develop when an elephant suddenly detects danger within its "critical distance", as the animal may then feel that its only option is a desperate charge. In reasonably open country, where there is time to take a good, if quick, aim, a charging elephant is not a terribly dangerous problem. Even if a shot between or just above the eyes does not kill, it should go close enough to the brain to stun the beast, at least momentarily.

In close cover, though, a wounded bull is a decidedly sticky proposition. An elephant can go through incredibly thick underbrush as though it were meadow grass. The hunter may see nothing but trees and branches crashing down towards him until the elephant bursts through the flying debris right over his head, giving him time for one, hastily-directed shot. Under these conditions the heaviest artillery will enhance one's chances of survival to some degree, but nothing will unfailingly stop an elephant if its brain is missed by more than a very few inches.

113

AAGAARD'S AFRICA

In the old days lions killed more hunters in Kenya than did any of the other dangerous game, partly because those who survived the mauling would die anyway of septicemia. Sulpha drugs changed that and since World War II fewer lions have been hunted by inexperienced men. I have not kept close count, but right off I can recall three hunters who have been killed by elephants in recent decades, as opposed to one each by lion, buffalo and rhino.

One of the three was a Kenya professional hunter whose lady client insisted that he should not collaborate on her elephant. She put two shots into a big bull, which nevertheless disappeared into a tangle of brush and trees. After escorting the lady back to the safari car, the hunter and his tracker went into the thicket after the jumbo, the hunter carrying his .577 Nitro Express double rifle. A lot of noise and a couple of shots were heard, then the horrified tracker came running back to report that his employer had been blotted out. (My journal comments, "Any client who wants to avoid my collaboration on dangerous game must drop it in its tracks with his first shot!")

The brain shot on elephant has quite aptly been likened to trying to hit a loaf of bread suspended inside a 50-gallon drum. The brain sits at the back of the skull and a line drawn from earhole to earhole would pass nearly through the center of it. The old advice to hold halfway between the eye and the ear for the side brain shot directs the bullet too far forward; it ought to get the front of the brain, but allows little leeway. I think it better to hold for the earhole itself or, depending on the angle, a few inches below it.

The frontal shot is trickier, because the brain is now end-on, presenting a smaller target, and is deeper in the head. Thus, it is farther removed from the external reference points that one may use to gauge its position. Considerable allowances may have to be made for the angle, depending on how close one is and how the elephant is holding its head. "Karamoja" Bell wrote that the best advice he could give those attempting the brain shot was to

114

A HUNTER REMEMBERS

shoot for the *exact center* of things, and hope everything works.

The elephant's heart and lungs present a larger vital area that is easier to hit than its brain. As with most mammals, a shot placed so as to pass through the center of the chest cavity between the front legs, and a good third of the depth of the chest up from the brisket, will get the top of the heart or the great blood vessels arising from it. So hit, an elephant will generally go down within 50 to 150 yards. The bullet should not be allowed to strike any distance behind the front leg on a broadside shot, as it is then quite easy to miss the lungs altogether. An elephant cannot jump, nor can it travel on three legs, so a shot that breaks the humerus or the shoulder joint definitely anchors it. I am uncertain whether cartridges smaller than the .375 H & H have the necessary power to fracture these very heavy bones, as it was the legal minimum for use on dangerous game in Kenya and I have no experience with lesser cartridges on elephant. Strongly constructed, full-metal-jacket, or "solid" bullets are, in any case, the only type that should be used on elephant, in order to obtain the requisite penetration.

Naturally, there are rare exceptions. With the bigger bores it would be possible to use heavy, soft-nose bullets for broadside chest shots, if care was taken to avoid massive bones. A school mate of mine brought down a tusker with the side brain shot using a soft-nose 175-gr. bullet in a 7x57 mm. But whether it would have stayed down is uncertain, as his companion immediately hammered it twice with a .470 Nitro Express. Actually, on the side brain shot there is not a great thickness of bone to penetrate, so a stout soft-point might get through.

Elephants range through a wide variety of habitats, from the arid thorn brush and doum palm country of the northern Uaso Nyiro (where the Samburu tribesmen still remember the great ivory hunter Neumann by his native name of "Nyama Nyangu" — literally "my meat"), to the gray scrub of the Tana River district, to the damp forests and bamboo thickets fringing the moorlands 10,000 feet up on the slopes of Mt. Kenya.

115

Consequently, one has to adapt his hunting methods to suit the circumstances of the particular hunt.

The classic method of hunting elephant is to track big-footed bulls up from their night's drinking spot at a river or waterhole. It seems to be *de riguer* to track them 20 miles out, and then march 20 miles back, at least; seldom does anyone admit to taking a shorter stroll after elephant. Actually, there are darned few visiting sportsmen (and, in truth, not many professionals) who could make even the first 20 miles in the heat common to most good elephant country. But the jumbos can go a lot farther than that if they have to. One year when it was exceptionally dry and the browse near the river had all been eaten out, we started tracking a lone bull from a bush road that ran parallel to the river, but 10 miles inland. When we caught up with the elephant, about noon, he was a good 20 miles from water and was still marching away from it. A bull will travel 30 or more miles from water and remain several days without drinking if things come to that.

Apart from checking watering spots, one can criss-cross elephant country looking for tracks or the beasts themselves, or spot them from the ridges and rocky outcroppings that are a feature of the Voi and Tsavo areas and of much of the Northern Frontier District (I acquired my first spotting scope for the specific purpose of ascertaining whether or not distant elephant herds contained ivory worth pursuing). Local tribesmen may be able to give information, especially if their crops are being raided (though to them all elephants carry huge ivory), or they may be employed as scouts and sent to search in all directions, with the promise of a suitable reward for news leading to a big bull. Or, quite likely, a combination of such tactics may be used.

The capabilities of the hunter have some bearing on the matter, too. One of my favorite clients was a chap who had flown Messerschmitt Me 109 fighters for Yugoslavia against the Germans during World War II and who afterwards, being no communist, settled at Graz in Austria. Sasha was a perfect

116

gentleman with graceful and charming European manners, a gifted raconteur and a delightful companion in every way. But, he had both diabetes and a bad heart. He was not supposed to walk for more than 30 minutes at time and slowly at that. His wife, Mickey, always came with him to see that he did not overdo it. And, naturally, he wanted an elephant very badly.

Hunting along the Tana River, below Garissa, we found where a small group of bulls had drunk during the night. One set of footprints were of promising size, so we decided to track them up. I sent Kinuno and a local we had hired ahead to follow the spoor, while Sasha, Mickey and I followed behind, bashing through the brush in the Land Rover. Towards midday I stopped, for fear the elephants might be alarmed by the sound of the motor, and sent the trackers on to find the jumbos while I gave Sasha and Mickey some lunch. Three hours later the local came back and said Kinuno was watching the bulls, who were taking their noontime siesta in the shade of a thicket. We drove on for another mile or two and then had to leave the vehicle. The guide said the elephants were close. We walked slowly for 20 minutes in the searing dry heat and the guide said the elephants were close. Sasha struggled gamely along without any complaint, but Mickey was beginning to look worried. After 30 minutes she caught my arm and asked how much farther we had to go and the guide said the elephants were close. After 40 minutes, Mickey insisted that we could not continue, and even Sasha had to admit that he was about done in. The guide said that the elephants were very close, just beyond that little rise ahead of us, so we went on and at last found Kinuno, who led us into the thicket where the bulls were resting.

The faint breeze in our faces carried the pungent, exhilarating odor of fresh elephant droppings and, as we crept in closer, I heard the smack of a fanning ear against a shoulder and a slight stir as an animal shifted its weight from one foot to another. In the middle of the thicket was a little glade and there we found our elephants standing under a wide-spreading, flat-topped thorn tree. Two were just young bulls, but the third carried thin but very long and even tusks. I told Sasha they would go perhaps 60 pounds a side at the most, but that with their length they would make a beautiful trophy, and he replied that was quite good enough.

We eased in a little closer, then Kinuno set up the crossed shooting sticks, giving Sasha a place to rest the fore-end of his .375. I watched the two young bulls, because one can never be quite certain what their reaction will be, and they were so close that any attempted charge would have to be stopped immediately. But at Sasha's shot they turned and fled, as they nearly always do. I saw the dust fly from our bull's shoulder as the bullet thwacked home. The animal wheeled and disappeared before Sasha could shoot again, but presently we heard a great crashing of brush and the sounds of a dying elephant. We found the bull, dead, less than 100 yards away.

The tusks were 7½ feet long, beautifully shaped and even, and weighed exactly 66 pounds apiece. Sasha was delighted. He had worked himself to his absolute limit and he deserved them. But, as Robert Ruark observed, a dead elephant is a grievous amount of death. I loved to hunt elephants, but lordy how I hated to kill one of them.

That was 20 years ago, when the Tana River area was, arguably, the best elephant country in Africa. Seven years later it was finished, with not an elephant or even a track to be seen anywhere, poached clean by Somali ivory raiders, many of them armed with automatic weapons. Rather than make any genuine attempt to stop the illegal slaughter, the Kenya government merely stopped licensed elephant hunting, and then, a short while later, stopped all legal hunting.

It has been downhill since then. Now in Kenya the elephants are gone from the Tana and the Athi, Tsavo and Galana rivers and from all the country between them. They are gone from the Ndotos and the Mathews range, from the Barsoloi Lugga and from all that great sweep of the Northern Frontier District up to

A HUNTER REMEMBERS

fabulous Mt. Marsabit with its Paradise Lake, where Martin and Osa Johnson camped. It may be possible to preserve a few small populations in some of the national parks where they can be heavily guarded, but that seems to be the best we can hope for. And it appears that within a few years the same could to be true for the rest of Africa as well. This saddens me immensely, for though I would never willingly kill an elephant again, a world in which there were no elephants — or elephant hunters — is not one I would care much for.

12

The Gray Ghost

To many people the greater kudu, with its magnificent spiraling horns and its regal bearing, is the most beautiful and desirable of all the African antelopes.

South West Africa, now known as Namibia, is the place in which to hunt greater kudu. There they are among the most numerous of the large antelope and are as much a nuisance and a danger to motorists as whitetail deer are in central Texas — or so they say. In fact, there is virtually no part of sub-Saharan Africa in which kudu do not dwell. Their range extends from a little below the Congo river in Angola, through Namibia, South Africa, Botswana, Mozambique and Zimbabwe; then up the eastern half of the continent through Zambia, Tanzania, Kenya, Somalia, and Ethiopia to the fringes of the Red Sea Hills, whence it hooks back through the southern Sudan to parts of Chad and the Central African Republic — a grand sweeping arc that traverses between seven and eight thousand miles of Africa.

Although habitat loss has reduced their numbers over much of this range, and the guerilla wars that ravage back and forth across Angola, Mozambique, Chad and Ethiopia have no doubt taken an added toll, kudu have been brought back in South Africa, are still plentiful in Zimbabwe, Botswana and Zambia, and are relatively common in Tanzania.

AAGAARD'S AFRICA

Common they may be in terms of population, but no one will ever accuse the kudu of being commonplace. A mature greater kudu bull weighs some 600-700 pounds and stands a good five feet tall at the shoulder, which is to say that it is not significantly smaller than the average Rocky Mountain bull elk. Kudu bulls are a blue-gray color with a white chevron between the eyes and six to 10 vertical white stripes on their flanks. Their ears are large, while their hooves are surprisingly small for the size of the beast, a not uncommon family characteristic among the *tragelaphine*, or spiral-horned, antelopes. (One exception is the swamp-dwelling sitatunga, with its greatly elongated hooves.)

Kudu appear almost slender compared to the burly roan and sable antelopes which, combined with their aristocratic bearing and the incredible grandeur of their horns, puts them among the most handsome and elegant animals on earth.

The heavy, ridged horns typically make two to two and one-half complete spirals and may tower to four feet above the head. According to Rowland Ward they are properly measured along the outside surface, and not around the spiral. The longest set on record, to my knowledge, is listed in the 1922 edition of Rowland Ward's *Records Of Big Game* measuring 71½ inches on the outside curve and 51¾ inches in a straight line from tip to base. A photo of this head, taken by J. Cole Rous (or Rouse) in the Lyndenburg district of the Transvaal, is included in that edition. It looks quite stupendous!

The East African greater kudu have smaller heads, on average, than the southern race and are listed separately in the record book. The minimum lengths for inclusion in "the book" used to be 49 inches for East African kudu and about 56 inches for the southern species.

Kudu are animals of the dry brush country and in general seem to prefer hilly terrain. They are principally browsers. The big bulls run in little bachelor bands or, very often, are solitary. Cows and younger animals are normally found in groups of four to six, though larger herds have been reported.

A HUNTER REMEMBERS

In addition to their large ears and love of cover, kudu share other traits with America's whitetail deer. Kudu are skulkers and hiders who depend more on concealment than on fleetness of foot and the way in which one can disappear in a patch of skimpy, leafless bush is uncanny.

Kudu also seem to have extraordinarily keen hearing, a good sense of smell and excellent eyesight. Like whitetail, they have quick and nervously alert dispositions, and at the first hint of trouble an old bull is likely to lay its horns down along its back and sneak away into a thicket before a hunter has any inkling of its presence.

Greater kudu were quite rare in Kenya and were found only in scattered pockets. For many years there was no open season on them, but eventually it was realized that the population was stable and could tolerate a carefully limited harvest.

Kenya's kudu inhabited an area in the Narok district of the Masai country. I have seen them in the canyon of the Siapei and above Narosura where the road winds steeply up into the Loita Hills. They were also to be found around the gorge where the southern Uaso Nyiro plunges down into the Great Rift Valley and farther north along the eastern wall of the Rift, particularly on the Laikipia escarpment above Lake Hannington. But for the most part we hunted them in the steep, hot, rocky hills of the arid Northern Frontier District. We climbed and glassed for them in country that looked like parts of Arizona and in many ways the hunting resembled that described in accounts of hunting the desert bighorn sheep.

A lot of African trophies, particularly the antelope, are collected by chance; one happens upon them while hunting something else. This was seldom the case with kudu in Kenya. They required a serious quest that concentrated on them exclusively and even seeing one was an event.

I first hunted them on Ray Mayer's Pyramid Ranch (named for a solitary hill of that shape) in the Loldiaga range to the northwest of Mt. Kenya.

AAGAARD'S AFRICA

There was a drought that year in the Loldiagas, in fact, there had not been a drop of rain in 11 months, and the country was burned up. I climbed the hills behind Ray's house in the black pre-dawn every day for a week, and glassed and searched both high and low 'til near dark. I saw several cows and a young bull with but one curl, but never a sign of the half-a-dozen mature bulls that normally ranged the property. It turned out that there had been a heavy, localized thunderstorm up to the north near Dol Dol a week or two previously and it is likely that they had migrated over there for the new browse.

I saw the young bull every day. It lived near the house and was so naive and used to people that I got close enough to have potted it with a .22. But what possible satisfaction could there have been in bagging it under those circumstances, even if it had had a shootable head?

Some years later Laird Mooney and I hunted kudu at Dol Dol while Ken Clark guided his uncle, Chip Loomis. After three days of hard hunting, during which we got only a fleeting glimpse of one small party of cows, we spotted a solitary bull high up on a hill. We went around behind the hill, dodging a bunch of agitated elephant on the way, climbed it, and crawled cautiously and expectantly until we could see over the crest. The kudu was nowhere to be seen.

There was a brushy draw running part way down the otherwise open slope. I left Laird and Kinuno where they had a commanding view and walked noisily down one side of the draw, allowing my scent to drift into it. It was a good guess, for presently the kudu burst out of the brush perforce into the open and Laird nailed it at a range of about 200 yards with the third shot from his .375 H & H. It proved to be a candidate for the record book, with spiralling horns that measured 51 inches along the outside curve.

There was a total eclipse of the sun that afternoon, but it seemed a minor event to us. Laird and I will always remember that day as "The Day We Shot The Kudu".

A HUNTER REMEMBERS

The next day Chip and Ken collected another beauty, with 47-inch horns, but a much wider spread. Getting two kudu in two days in Kenya was fantastic and, if memory serves, we bagged a record-book Grant's gazelle and gerenuk during the same hunt, so altogether we did rather well.

The other main kudu hunting ground in Kenya lay just to the south of Lake Turkana (formerly Lake Rudolph) in Hunting Block 52, which included Ol Donyio Nyiro (roughly, "The Dark Mountain") and some isolated, rough-hewn hills with names like Kowop, Koitokol and Sartin.

Block 52 was home to the Butterfly People, the Samburu who are close kin to the Masai, to the camel-herding Rendille and to the wild Turkana. The block was also home to big, narrow-striped Grevy's zebra, the hardy and courageous beisa oryx with their lance-like horns and flowing tails, the long-necked gerenuk that stand up on their hind legs to delicately nibble acacia leaves, a few rhino, some big-tusked elephants. And, in the wooded valleys that tumbled down the sides of Mt. Nyiro, there lived a surprising number of leopards .

Don Siebern and I (accompanied by my wife and our six-month-old son) camped under the flat-topped thorn trees by the Uaso Rongai, a stream at the south end of Nyiro, and hung leopard baits all around. While awaiting a nibble, we hunted kudu on the nearer reaches of the mountain and nearby hills.

There was a Samburu village nearby and naturally the women flocked to our camp to satisfy their curiosity about the white woman, and more particularly the white baby, something they had never seen. One old lady came every day to watch young Erik being bathed and always asked the same question about something that seemed to concern her gravely. I had brought along a young Masai lad to act as interpreter, but we always took him out hunting with us, so it was not until we came in early one day that Berit was able to discover what was troubling her visitor.

Did Berit suckle the child, she demanded to know, having

apparently heard horror stories about white women feeding their infants junk out of cans. Her face lightened when Berit assured her that she did so, but then clouded again with doubt. How could she when she wore clothes that covered her upper body? Berit had to unbutton her blouse and demonstrate, and then the old crone finally went away happy and relieved.

It was again an unusually dry year, even for that semi-desert country, and we went several days without seeing any fresh sign of kudu, though Don did collect a good oryx. It was an almost toothless old beast with suppurating lion claw marks on its face and neck.

Eventually we found a good kudu bull taking his midday siesta in the shade near the top of Kowop Hill. The wind was such that the only possible approach was up a little gully. We ended up crawling on hands and knees, but ran out of cover more than 400 yards below our quarry. The kudu had noticed something and was staring in our direction, but it was still too far to shoot. So Kinuno and I sat there, talking casually and never looking at the kudu, while Don got down on his belly and by slithering along like a snake successfully worked his way to a rocky ledge perhaps 75 yards closer.

He put his hat in a notch in the rock, rested the rifle on it, wriggled around until he was comfortable, took unhurried aim and fired. But at the shot there was a puff of dust just under the kudu's brisket and that was the end of that. We had simply underestimated the range and consequently the amount of hold-over required.

A few years later Lowell Douglas and I came back, strictly for kudu. This time we camped at Tuum, a one-store trading post on the western side of Nyiro, intending to concentrate our hunting on the mountain. We sought information among the locals and finally one of the Samburu said that he could show us a place on the mountain to the north of Tuum where a *big* bull — he raised both arms high over his head to illustrate — used to live. That country was now uninhabited, he explained, because the previous year a band of renegade Shifta had moved through it, killed the people and made off with their livestock.

At the next morning's first light, Lowell, Kinuno and I, together with the Samburu guide and a pal of his whom he insisted on having along, left the Toyota at the end of the track and started climbing. We went slowly — because Lowell had two crippled knees that he had injured playing college basketball — and we stopped at every suitable point to search the ground with binoculars. Our hearts leaped when, soon after leaving the truck, we startled a big, gray antelope out of a thicket. But it was only an eland bull that went away, its dewlap swinging from side to side, in the smooth, ground-eating trot that is characteristic of the breed.

Towards midday it became obvious that Lowell's knees were giving him considerable pain and that he was about done. I decided we would make one last spy from the next little rise and then turn back.

It was Kinuno who sidled to the crest and peeked over, then slid back from it and signaled for me to come up beside him. Across the valley, a thousand yards away in the shade of a scraggly thorn tree, lay a kudu bull.

From that distance I could not tell how big the bull really was, but its horns showed the two full curls of a mature animal and that was plenty good enough for us.

Unfortunately, there was no way to approach it from where we were without being seen. The proper thing to have done would have been to go back down the mountain the way we had come, make our way around behind the main ridge, climb it and come at the kudu from above. But that would have necessitated a hard march of several hours over rough terrain and Lowell's knees would have given out completely before we had covered even half the distance.

Groups of people walking from hither to yon across country are a common sight in East Africa. So in the end I decided that we would just stroll openly up our ridge, talking and showing no interest in the kudu, until we reached a spot opposite it from which Lowell would have a long, but feasible, shot. There, he was to drop down behind a tree while the rest of us walked on and do the best he could.

Of course it did not work, which is just as well. As soon as we came in view, the kudu rose to its feet. Then it turned and went slowly up the hill, stopping to stare back at us from time to time — a beautiful sight with the sun glinting off those great horns — until it disappeared into what appeared to be a little basin on the crest of the ridge, overlooked by a rocky knoll.

Though unsuccessful on its surface, our ploy had succeeded to the extent that the kudu had not seemed unduly alarmed, and I thought that there was a fair chance that it might stop and bed down again in the high basin. I suggested that we should continue up our ridge for another half-mile, then cross the valley to the main ridge and come down it until we could look into the basin from the knoll. Lowell was tired and hurting, but he gamely assented to give it a try.

It took us an hour, but finally we reached the rocky knoll and climbed it. After a break to catch our breath, I put Kinuno in the lead, closely followed by Lowell, who had instructions to be ready to shoot quickly if the kudu broke cover.

Suddenly Kinuno stopped, touched Lowell's arm, and pointed. The two Samburu immediately sprang forward to get a better look, but I was able to grab them in time. Lowell stared where Kinuno pointed, nodded, moved a step to his right as if to get a clearer view, snugged the .270 into his shoulder and fired.

"GOT HIM!" I rushed up, saw the kudu thrashing on the ground, realized it had dropped out of Lowell's sight and slapped a .375 bullet into it to be sure it would not get up. It proved an unnecessary precaution.

Lowell said the kudu had been standing in the thorn brush about 60 yards away, looking at him. Its chest had been completely obscured, leaving him no option but to shoot it in the neck, which he had done as nicely as you please.

A HUNTER REMEMBERS

Then came the hard work. We had to skin it and cut it up, carry it down off the mountain and then about three miles out to the Toyota. But, who cared? I was glad to be staggering along with the heavy horns gouging my shoulders, the blood trickling down my back and the sweat-bees swarming around my face!

That kudu was a real trophy, no matter what it measured. In fact, I never did put a tape to it because it seemed entirely beside the point. (I believe it is listed in the Safari Club book, though.) We had done it right and Lowell had given it everything he had to give, and then some. He thoroughly deserved his success.

As for me, I have never taken an East African greater kudu "to my own gun" and likely never will. But I have enjoyed the signal privilege of being allowed to hunt them and with fine companions by and large, and that is enough.

13

Buffalo Encounters

If you were to ask him, Ronnie Berman, who runs one of Houston's best restaurants, would probably tell you that there is nothing much to hunting buffalo — a chap simply goes a little way out of camp and shoots one.

When Ronnie came on safari with us in 1976 he had never fired a shot at any sort of four-footed game whatsoever. But Leonard Burke, his mentor and companion on the hunt, had taken him out to the range many times, and had so drilled and practiced him that Ronnie handled a rifle safely and very competently. He shot quite well, too, even with the .375 H & H Magnum that Len lent him.

We made our first camp in the cool forests of the rolling Loita Hills; at the edge of the trees overlooking a long open valley near Entasekera, at about 7,000 feet elevation. We arrived in mid-afternoon, and by 5:00 p.m. were all settled in, camp pitched, the rifles sighted in and afternoon tea quaffed. I suggested that we might drive around a little to get the feel of the country and perhaps find tracks or other indications that would give us some hint as to where we should start hunting on

131

the morrow. Almost as an afterthought, I suggested that we might as well take our rifles along with us.

Kinuno stood in the back of the Land Rover station wagon with his head out of the roof hatch, but the rest of us were not paying much attention. Len and I were reminiscing, for Ronnie's benefit, about our first hunt together, some five years previously. Then, Len had been the neophyte and a smallish zebra that we bagged the opening morning of the hunt was the very first game animal larger than a rabbit that he had ever taken. But, by the end of a wonderful three-week safari he was a veteran, with two buffalo and an elephant to his credit, and both he and his vivacious wife, Connie, had fallen so much in love with Africa that they had come back to some part of it every year since.

"*Sumama, Bwana — Nyati!*" Kinuno urgently and accusingly broke in on our yakking, commanding me to stop because he had seen a buffalo. Sure enough. A patch of forest grew along the crest of the otherwise open ridge across the valley from our position and a huge, grizzled, old buffalo bull had emerged from the trees to graze in the open during the cool of the evening. The massiveness of its horns was quite apparent even to the naked eye and I did not have to study it for long before reaching a decision.

"Darn it," I said to Ronnie, "I had planned to break you in gently on an impala or something equally innocuous, but that fellow is much too good for us to pass up. Bring the .375 and follow me."

Luckily, our side of the valley was timbered, so we just went straight down it under cover and started up the other side. Though it was open grassland, the opposite slope was so convex that we could see no more than about 30 yards ahead. Nearing the top, we went very slowly until I caught a flicker of movement up ahead. It was the bull, swishing his tail at an insect. I grabbed Ronnie's arm and motioned for him to imitate my crouch as we duck-walked forward another 20 feet. Then we

132

stood up quickly, while with practiced swiftness Kinuno planted the crossed shooting sticks in front of Ronnie and indicated that he should lay the rifle in the crotch. The surprised bull raised his head to stare, standing with his body turned almost but not quite straight towards us, and startled into a fleeting immobility. I touched Ronnie on the collar bone, between neck and shoulder.

"Hit it right there," I commanded in a whisper. "Shoot now!"

I hardly heard the roar of the .375, but was astounded to see the bull simply collapse and roll over with all four feet in the air when the 300-gr. Winchester "solid" bullet thumped home. It was so unexpected — buffalo never drop in their tracks — that I must have stood there gaping for almost a whole second before remembering to tell Ronnie to shoot it again, as is customary and wise. It was redundant in this case, but old professionals don't attain that status by taking unnecessary chances.

The whole episode was utterly incredible. This kid, on his first afternoon out of Nairobi, rides for 20 minutes in the Land Rover, walks perhaps half a mile and clobbers a monstrous old buffalo, which just rolls over in its tracks, as dead as the proverbial kippered herring. Not only is it the first game of any sort he has ever taken, but it is also a tremendous trophy, with massive bosses and deep curls that sweep around to give a 43½-inch spread. Many a man has spent weary weeks of travail on several different safaris looking for a decent buffalo without getting anything nearly as good.

Later in the hunt we spent most of two days trying to get a shot at one particularly handsome, and very elusive, impala buck. So Ronnie might tell you that buffalo are a piece of cake, but that impala are a real challenge. Not everyone would agree with him, of course, in fact hardly anyone would. Len certainly knew better, as we had a trifling amount of excitement with the two buffalo taken on his original hunt.

We encountered the first one on a bench half way down into the gorge of the Siapei, a stream that meanders through the Narok district. Len hit it hard with my .375, and I slapped a .458

slug into its departing backside. Despite our efforts, it got into a thicket and we spent a slightly hair-raising 10 minutes following it up before we heard its death bellow. Then we moved most of the way across Kenya to the hot, dry, low-altitude thorn scrub of the Galana country, that in many ways resembles West Texas.

Mainly we were after elephant, lesser kudu and oryx, but one evening we spotted three big buffalo bulls wandering along a *lugga*. One of them appeared to be significantly better than Len's first buffalo, so we made a fast stalk to get in front of them. Our timing was perfect. As we reached the *lugga* we saw them browsing slowly along; huge, gray, menacingly solid forms that were intermittently visible through the brush as they advanced irresistibly upon us. Eventually the big fellow, accompanied by one of the lesser bulls, came out into the clear, not 25 yards from where we stood.

Len hit it just in front of the shoulder joint and the 300-gr. Kynoch "solid" went clear through and smashed the last rib on the far side. The bull stumbled, then broke into a hard run in the direction it was pointed, which was towards us. I slammed a 500-gr. "solid" from the .458 into it, turning it enough that Len's second shot took it through the chest close behind the shoulders. That slowed it down visibly, so I was able to divert my attention to the second bull, circling around behind us, head high and with a wild look about its eyes. For a few seconds I really thought that I might have to shoot it, something I was loath to do for, apart from any other consideration, we were out of buffalo licenses. But fortunately when I shouted at it — using rather uncouth language, I am afraid — it took the hint and went away.

Bulls are commonly found in small bachelor groups, the members of which are usually quite obviously buddies. My brother-in-law, Peter Davey, saw and photographed an incident in which a buffalo bull charged and, temporarily at least, drove off a pack of a dozen lions that were attacking another bull. The victim was too far gone to escape, however, and in the end the

A HUNTER REMEMBERS

lions came back and pulled it down. Some of Peter's shots of the episode appeared in an issue of *Life Magazine* many years ago.

I witnessed a similar occurrence in the Masai Mara game reserve. We came across five young adult lions who were harassing a lone buffalo bull. One of them would feint at its head while the others sneaked around behind it, apparently trying to hamstring it. They had bitten the bull's tail off and had ripped the hide on its haunches into bloody shreds, but had not yet managed to cripple it, when another buffalo bull appeared on the scene. It immediately went for the big cats and chased them off. The lions withdrew to a large tree half a mile away and flopped down in the shade, while the two buffalo took refuge in a thicket. For the rest of the day the unhurt bull remained with its companion, charging out furiously at any car or tourist bus that came too close.

I was never charged by the buddy of a bull we had just shot, but on several occasions it seemed that one of them may have been seriously considering doing so and I have no doubt at all that it could happen.

In fact it did happen — in 1970, according to a yellowed cutting from the *East African Standard* that is in my journal — to professional hunter Boet Dannhauser. It seems that local tribesmen had asked Dannhauser and his partner, Doug Coetzee, to deal with a group of several buffalo bulls that were raiding their corn fields every night. The two hunters tracked the buffalo to a patch of brush where they were lying up and then had the tribesmen throw stones into the thicket to drive them out.

One bull came rushing out past Coetzee, who bowled it over with a fine shot. Nothing further developed, so Dannhauser entered the bush, walking along a little stream, to find out whether the rest had cleared off. Rounding a bend, he came face to face with a great bull that immediately charged him. Boetie gave it both loads from his double-barrel .458, shooting from the hip, and then tried to leap aside, but the buffalo hit his knee and

135

knocked him down. As he fell, the bull hooked a horn under his belt and tossed him in the air, ripping off both the belt and his shorts and leaving him in what would have been an embarrassing state of *dishabille* if he had had time to worry about it.

Dannhauser had been wearing a revolver. Somehow he managed to grab it before he lost his belt and he landed on his feet with the handgun in his fist. The bull charged in once more. Boetie shot in desperation with the handgun. The bull knocked him down into the stream and held him under water until he managed to wriggle free, shoot it again, and drive it away.

The newspaper reported that Dannhauser said, "The revolver saved me, and the fact that if I lay still the buffalo would do the same. When I moved he would charge."

Dannhauser drove off the bull several times and was down to the last cartridge in the cylinder before Coetzee was able, at terribly long last, to get to the scene and shoot the beast off him. Incredibly, Boetie sustained no worse damage than a couple of broken ribs and the thing that apparently impressed him most about the encounter was that the bull had had the cheek to "de-bag" him.

Normally, however, one would not expect any trouble unless he was following up a beast that had been bashed, but not too well. My tracker, Kinuno, almost met bad trouble once under those circumstances. Matters began to go wrong from the very beginning when, through a misunderstanding, Dr. Ed Rizk shot the smaller of two bulls in a bunch instead of the larger one. The wounded animal wheeled around and went lumbering away after the others in that ponderous, rocking-horse canter of theirs. I managed to get a .458 bullet into its mid-section somewhere and then the brush closed around it. For a little while we could hear them crashing through the shrubbery, then all fell quiet. We waited hopefully for the mournful bellows a dying buffalo often emits, but there was only an ominous silence. It became obvious that we were going to have to poke around in that nasty thick stuff to learn if the bull was dead, or merely very vexed.

A HUNTER REMEMBERS

We started to follow the spoor in, but then it occurred to me that might not be the thing to do. Instead we skirted around the thicket and entered it 50 yards downwind from the tracks. Proceeding very slowly and alertly, pausing every few feet to look and listen, and ducking down frequently to peer under the brush in the hope of spotting legs, we eventually came out into a tiny glade. By then, I was convinced that the wounded bull must have gone on with the herd, so I sent Kinuno ahead to search for their tracks while Ed and I stayed back out of his way. All at once there was a furious grunting and Kinuno came flying back, hurdling low bushes and fallen limbs in fine style, with the buffalo close behind him and gaining.

We threw up our rifles, but Kinuno and the buffalo were in line and we could not shoot. For a few everlasting, horrifying moments it seemed that we would be forced to watch helplessly while the buffalo caught and tossed him. Fortunately, Kinuno became aware of the problem and swerved abruptly to his left. At a range of 10 feet Ed and I fired simultaneously into the bull's shoulder. It went down as if under a pile driver, but I poured two more shots into it anyway. Incidentally, Ed got on to the buffalo at this short range just as quickly using the 2½X Weaver scope on the .375 as I was able to do with the iron-sighted .458.

We got away with it that time, but I believe that fully a quarter of the professional hunters in Kenya had been pounded on by a buffalo at one time or another. Surprisingly enough, though, I can only remember one fatality, Tony Catchpole.

Tony was Kenya born and raised. After serving in the British army, where he attained the rank of Major, he decided to go into the safari business. He was hunting buffalo near Lolgorien, in western Masailand, in order to gain the experience necessary to qualify for a professional hunter's license. Exactly what happened is uncertain, but I gather that when they spotted a large, solitary bull buffalo that was a known rogue, Catchpole jumped out of the Land Rover and went after it, carrying a double rifle but no spare ammunition. He fired both of the cartridges he had in the rifle and then the buffalo caught him.

In truth, however, charges are rare and very few visiting hunters ever experience a genuine, deadly charge *a' outrace*. While buffalo hunts are seldom exactly routine, one might say that the majority are relatively uneventful.

Take Bill Keith's buffalo as an example. Sunrise in the Loita Hills found us working our way up the crest of a long ridge when a large, dark-pelted forest leopard crossed close in front of us. It stopped to snarl its resentment at our intrusion while the low sun spotlighted it against the green grass, a gorgeous sight. Only a few hundred yards farther on we caught a glimpse of some buffalo moving just beyond the next little rise. We made a rapid sneak up to a little clump of trees and there they were, six or seven buffalo bulls walking slowly past us at about 50 paces and disappearing one by one into the black shadows of the forest beyond.

Bill already had one fairly decent buffalo, so he was only interested in an exceptional head. But when the second from last came by I did not need to hesitate.

"That's a very good one, Bill. Shoot it!"

Inevitably, the bull plunged into the thick stuff. But I had seen the bullet strike and it had looked good. A couple of minutes later we heard a few low, moaning bellows.

"I believe that you killed it," I told Bill, "but we can't be absolutely certain of that, so we will proceed as if we knew it to be wounded."

It took us a tense 30 minutes or more to cover the 60 yards it had run down the slope. It was quite dead when we reached it, probably just as well, for it was so thick in there that I almost trod on the buffalo's tail before I saw the animal.

And then there was the "Wild Kongoni Gang". It consisted of the notorious Frank Kongoni himself, aided and abetted by Wild Bill Warthog. (When they flew F4 Phantom jets for the U.S. Air Force they were also known as Capt. John McCoy and Major William B. Adams, respectively.) The gang had harried far and

Hunters going into the N.F.D. from Barsaloi either walk or travel as part of a government camel train. Caravan operators provide animals and handlers, like these sturdy "cameleers", to load and carry cargo.

Dr. Herb Beutel, of Mesquite, Texas, went on a camel safari with us, looking especially to take a leopard. The result of his efforts was a nicely-figured Tom, downed using a Belgian Browning "Safari Grade" chambered for 7 mm Remington Magnum.

Leopards, unlike some large cats, are at home in trees, which they climb to feed, or rest, or watch over the surrounding area. We photographed one big Tom, up a yellow fever tree, probably for the latter purpose.

Just a couple of cowboys on a "busman's holiday". Drs. Herb Beutel (l.) and Joey Pirung (r.) went on a camel-pack safari, but opted to ride more familiar ponies instead of camels and took a groom to help with the chores.

The tape showed that "Sasha" Schwab's elephant's tusks ran 7 feet, 8 inches and 7 feet, 1 inch. They weighed 66 pounds each. Sasha (r.), suffering from heart disease and diabetes, worked at great risk to earn these trophies.

"Sasha" Schwab and his wife, Mickey, were among my most memorable clients. Sasha, a gentleman of the old school and an ardent sportsman, pushed himself beyond his usual physical limits to down his elephant.

East African greater kudu are shorter-horned than the southern subspecies. Of these heads, the one on the left measured 51 inches and qualified for Rowland Ward's **Records of Big Game**.

Jorg Butherer (above) hunted lion with my friend Soren Lindstrom and me. Butherer's only shot failed to anchor his cat and I had to use my .458 to end the affair.

US Air Force Capt. John McCoy (l.) took a fine rhino on our safari to the N.F.D. McCoy gave my friend and tracker, Kinuno, a major share of the credit for a successful hunt and a memorable trophy.

Leonard Burke had not hunted big game when he arrived for safari in 1971 but he had practiced on targets and was a competent rifleman. His first trophy was a one-shot kill.

The Burkes, Connie and Len, journeyed from Houston, Texas, to make his first African hunt. Len's success afield included a record-book Thompson's gazelle.

On one of our trips to the Narok District, two young Masai women insisted on being photographed with Berit. The "hands in front" pose is the polite way for expectant mothers (three of them) to stand, in Masai society.

Of all the animals I hunted, only this buffalo was a solo performance from start to finish. It brings a sense of satisfaction known only to hunters of dangerous game. Of all my trophies, only this one made the trip to Texas.

wide in the land, successfully making off with many a fine trophy, and now the last day found us on top of the Siria Escarpment with one unfilled buffalo license.

It was beautiful country, a high plateau overlooking the Mara River, with thickly forested valleys, open ridge tops and grassy plains sprinkled with small stands of trees and clumps of brush. It contained one of the very few herds of Roan antelope to be found in Kenya, and from our camp on the edge of the escarpment we could look out over the whole Mara Game Reserve and watch huge herds of several hundred buffalo that looked like swarms of ants far below us. It was a splendid hunting ground indeed. It was open enough that one could see, yet with enough cover for stalking; cool, because of its 6,000-foot elevation; and green, because the escarpment caught the rain. And it was full of buffalo.

We soon found a herd of about 40 moving slowly along the forest edge in a valley. The wind allowed us to get ahead of them and find an ambush position in the cover of some brush. A buffalo cow presently emerged into the open some 10 yards in front of us, closely followed by a young bull — not big enough to interest us — with sex on its mind. The youngster sniffed and nudged, but the cow would have none of it. All at once the cow lifted its nose suspiciously, then turned and bolted for the forest. Next we heard the whole herd stampeding down the valley. The forest ended a quarter-mile away, so we cut out onto the open slope above the trees and hurried after them.

Suddenly another smaller bunch of buffalo appeared about 70 yards above us on the open ridge, moving up the valley. I expect that they had been disturbed by the large herd crashing through the forest, but did not know where the danger lay. They had not seen us, so Wild Bill put his .375 up on the cross-sticks and waited. I told him to take the last bull in the bunch. The rifle crashed, the buffalo bucked as the bullet told, then it ran. In my usual fashion I managed to get a .458 "solid" into its rear end, just as it disappeared behind a patch of brush.

139

AAGAARD'S AFRICA

The herd went over the ridge. We reloaded and were about to follow them when the bull burst out of the brush and came thundering down the slope straight at us. I do not believe it was a deliberate charge. I think the bull found that it could not follow its companions and so was taking the most direct route to the sanctuary of the forest below. Of course, the distinction might have been somewhat academic for a person who was in its way.

Everyone opened rapid fire. It must have sounded like the action at Rorke's Drift all over again. But 1,500 pounds of buffalo thundering down hill as hard as it can go is awesomely difficult to stop, and it took nine or 10 hits before it swerved aside and dropped 20 paces away to our left. Even Kinuno got in a couple of shots with my .375, which absolutely made his day.

A year or two later I was back in the same area with just a couple of fellows to look after the camp, hunting buffalo for myself. It had occurred to me that I had never hunted buffalo entirely on my own, I had always had at least a local tribesman along to help me. Now I wanted to rectify that, purely for my own satisfaction. At the last moment a friend asked me to take an Australian visitor along, a city chap who wanted to see what it was all about. That did not fit in well with my plans, for he was a non-hunter who would be more hindrance than help, but I could not refuse.

We saw a lot of buffalo. I got into a nice herd of about 60 the first day and maneuvered until I had them all drifting past me, but there was not a shootable bull among them. Then I stalked a big lone bull and could have shot it several times, except that I was never able to get a good look at its horns, they were always hidden in the brush. In the end it went down the escarpment into the non-shooting area.

Early next morning while tracking another herd I came on four bulls in fairly open country and was able to stalk up on them, crawling on hands and knees through the dew-wet grass, for the last 50 yards. The largest of the four would do, it had well-formed horns with heavy bosses and a fair spread. It was

140

standing turned halfway towards me and was looking around alertly as if it had caught a faint hint of my scent. I rested my hand on the rock to steady the .375, and placed the crosshairs in the K2.5 Weaver scope on the forward edge of the bull's shoulder. At the shot all four buffalo ran and went behind a mott of trees and brush some 70 paces away. Likewise, all four reappeared on the other side of the trees, but then one of them turned back and staggered into the cover. Half a minute later the tops of the bushes shook violently and then came the buffalo's death bellows.

That evening, after butchering the animal and taking care of the meat, I took Roy, the Australian, for a drive along the edge of the escarpment. We found an outstandingly fine impala that was a candidate for the record book, but I let it be. Then we saw more buffalo, topi, waterbuck, zebra, lots of oribi and warthogs, giraffe and finally a small pack of six wild dogs — fascinating animals that were not often encountered.

The buffalo head had a spread of 42 inches, decent but in no way outstanding. But it will always hang over my fireplace and, of the few trophies I have kept, it is the only one that I care very much about. It is all mine, taken entirely by my own efforts, skill and luck, and I don't have to share it with anyone else.

The African (or Cape) Buffalo is not a rare species. In fact, it is by far the most common of the "Big Five", and must still number in the millions. Buffalo are not difficult to find, it is no big deal to see several hundred in a day in good country. They are not very difficult to approach, usually, despite having good vision and excellent noses. They are not even pretty. Buffalo are just ugly, dour, courageous great bovines that can take an incredible amount of punishment and still remain on their feet long enough to kill a man if he makes a mistake.

That is why true buffalo addicts do not hunt merely for the trophy. We hunted the black bulls for the sake of the hunting, for the excitement, and to test ourselves.

141

14

Hunting His Majesty

The first vulture came plummeting out of the hot, burnished-steel, noonday African sky, stretching its legs out to reach the ground and back-stroking desperately with cupped wings to break its fall. Vultures are superlatively graceful on the wing, consummate soarers, but they are clumsy on the ground and when one lands it resembles a crash more than it resembles any controlled enterprise.

As it thumped down the bird craned its neck and nervously twitched its head around in all directions. Finding all clear, it hopped awkwardly to the dead zebra and, after another look around, stabbed its sharp, hooked beak into the soft area between the hind legs.

A second vulture landed beside the first and then another. Within seconds the rest of the circling cloud was hurtling to earth and the zebra was hidden under a heaving, straining, frenzied mass of pecking birds. Tall, grotesquely ugly Marabou storks paced around the fringes of the crowd, ready to mug and rob any unfortunate vulture that attempted to retire from the fray with a choice morsel, while a handsome little silver-backed jackal came sneaking out of the grass to see what it could glean.

Soren Lindstrom, who had been watching both the show and the nearby lava flow intently through his binoculars, finally stood up, shook his head dejectedly and turned to his client.

"It is not going to work this time," he said, "those blasted *morani* scared the lions so badly that they will not come out into the open today for anything, not even to save that lovely, juicy zebra meat from the vultures."

Lions hate vultures. One of my more vivid memories is of a lioness, who had just chased a mob of them away from her kill, standing up on her hind legs and flailing with her front paws in an exasperated attempt to swat them out of the air. On the other hand, the big cats are lazy and unprincipled, opportunists who would just as soon pirate someone else's kill as make their own. A gathering of vultures will quite often bring lions hurrying in to see whether there is anything worth appropriating.

We had been seeking the lions for several days, but that morning a band of newly-fledged *morani* (young Masai warriors) had encountered and speared a couple of the juvenile members of the pride. The rest of the lions had taken refuge in one of the many brush-covered, and incredibly rough, ancient lava flows that run across the land like ribbons of spilt molasses in the area betweeen the volcanic Chuylu Hills and Tanzania's fabulous Mt. Kilimanjaro.

Every few years all male Masai youths of a suitable age undergo perhaps the most important rite of their lives when, after a period of rigorous tutelage and testing, they are circumcised and initiated into the warrior class. They go off to live in separate young warriors' villages (the Masai equivalent of military barracks), and in former times it was their duty and pride to raid neighboring tribes.

Nowadays spoil-sport authorities frown rather severely on that sort of thing, so lion hunting is one of the few ways left for the *morani* to demonstrate their prowess and win the adoration of the maidens.

A HUNTER REMEMBERS

It is by no means unknown for a Masai cattle-herder to kill a lion by himself, but most lion hunts are group affairs. Generally scouts are sent out to find a lion (or a small group of lions). The location is reported to the pig-tailed, red ocher-smeared, ostrich-plumed spearmen who begin by surrounding their prey, then close in from all sides until they stand shoulder to shoulder in an unbreakable ring of shields and spears.

Individual lions react differently to this exigency. Some will furiously charge one of the warriors in a determined bid to break through the circle. Then the *moran* crouches under his heavy buffalo-hide shield and endeavors to spear the lion as it rears up over him, while his companions on either side also hurl in their spears. In the end, the hunter who receives the charge will most likely find himself on the ground under his shield with a dying lion thrashing around on top of him and usually he collects some highly impressive scars to enhance his status.

On other occasions the lion refuses to charge, but only makes angry and noisy feints in various directions, as if uncertain of what it ought to do. Then, if a *moran* wants to earn the highest honor, he dashes in to grab the lion by the tail and hold it while his comrades spear the beast. I expect he hopes that they will be quick about it. Everyone is berserk with excitement, spears whistle about madly and the lion usually winds up looking like a feline pincushion.

Masai warriors apparently rate one lion as highly as any other and they have no qualms about killing a lioness, or a cub, if that is what they encounter. When he met them that morning, Soren learned from the *morani* that when they speared the two juvenile lions the rest of the pride, including a mature male, had evaded them and escaped into the lava. Soren took his Toyota hunting car slowly around the lava flow. When he caught a glimpse of the lions he did not alarm them further by stopping, driving, instead, out onto the open plain; where his client shot a zebra.

He hitched the zebra to the truck, dragged it back to where they had seen the lions and dropped it off. Then he took the

AAGAARD'S AFRICA

Toyota a mile away, and he and his client sneaked back on foot to see if the vultures would entice the lions to come out.

When it became apparent that the ploy was not going to succeed, Soren hitched the zebra behind his truck once more and dragged it up and down the length of the lava flow to leave a scent trail. Then, sure that the lions would scent the trail when they left their sanctuary to go and drink at the waterhole — which they were bound to do — Soren located a suitable tree in which to hang the bait.

The one he selected stood in a pocket on the edge of the lava, where a subsidiary ridge of rock ran out at an angle from the main flow to form a bay in the lava. On this "headland", which would provide useful cover for the approach, Soren built his blind. Possibly "blind" is too strong a word. He merely cleared sufficient space in a clump of scraggly thorn for four of us to sit and piled the cut vegetation up to form a screen on the side towards the bait. Two holes, barely large enough to aim through, were made in the screen. Then, he very carefully cleared all the leaves, twigs and loose stones away from the floor of the hide and from the path leading up to it. Then he marked the path with little pieces of toilet paper.

There is an art to hanging a lion bait. Soren put a rope around the zebra's neck and hauled it up into the tree with the Toyota until its hindquarters were four or five feet off the ground. There he tied it fast. He also made sure that there were no limbs left on which vultures could perch to reach the bait. Hyenas would be able to get at just enough of it to keep them whooping and giggling around it. If there is anything that attracts lions more surely than vultures, it is the sound of excited hyenas around a kill. By tying the bait at just that height, Soren arranged things so that the lions would be able to feed on most, but not quite all, of it. Enough would remain tantalizingly out of reach to hold them there until morning. Otherwise, a large pride can clean up a zebra and be several miles away by dawn.

While Soren was thus occupied I went off, at his request, to

146

A HUNTER REMEMBERS

hang a couple of additional baits around a likely looking swamp at the far end of the hunting block. I found no tracks or any other sign of lion activity in that vicinity and thus did not expect much result from them. In any event, they remained untouched. Although it is worthwhile to keep a check on the carcasses of recently-killed large animals such as elephants and buffalo, hanging lion baits at random is usually wasted effort. There are exceptions, but normally a bait is best used only after lions have been located and their likely movements have been deduced, when it serves mostly to hold them where one can get at them.

We left camp well before daybreak the next morning, parked the Toyota a good mile from the bait and made our way on foot towards the blind by the light of a quarter moon. Excitement started building when a lion suddenly began grunting from the general vicinity of the bait tree. Then, when we were within 100 yards of the bait, a lion called from between us and the blind, and was answered by another far away in the direction of the waterhole. There was no future in stumbling over lions in the dark, so we sat down and waited for it to get lighter. Even so, as we reached the blind a startled lion got up from directly below it and dashed for the lava flow.

"Damnation, that blew it!" was Soren's assessment.

But it struck me that the animal had looked small, like a half-grown cub, whose alarm might not be taken too seriously by the rest of the pride, so we settled into the blind to await further developments.

We didn't wait long. Just as the sun came up, a lioness materialized at the foot of the tree. It studied the remains of the bait, rose up on her hind legs, hooked a paw into the zebra's shoulder to steady herself and began to feed. Other lions followed, and for a quarter of an hour or so lionesses were continually moving back and forth between the bait and the lava flow. Now and again we caught glimpses of a lion with what appeared to be a fairly decent blond mane, but it remained in the background where we could not get a good look at it.

147

AAGAARD'S AFRICA

Finally a pretty young lioness left the bait, climbed up the lava ridge to our right and sat looking straight down into the blind from a distance of perhaps 30 feet. It had noticed something out of the way and stared for an eternity trying to make out what it was. It cocked its head first one way then another and then tried the old trick of turning away as if it had lost interest, only to snap its gaze back suddenly to catch any moment. We sat still as statues, but I felt its curiosity was such that eventually it would have to come down and stick its head into the blind to find out what we were.

Luckily another lioness distracted its attention by coming up to rub faces with it — just as domestic cats do — before flopping down in the sunshine a few yards away. After several other members of the pride had gone by to enjoy the same patch of warmth, our watcher gave up its vigil and joined them.

An older lioness, heavy in milk, took a slightly different route. It came up onto the ridge beside the blind and stopped not 10 feet from me, gazing out onto the plain beyond. As there were only a few leafless branches between us it could hardly have failed to have seen me, had it glanced in my direction, and to this day I am simply astounded that it did not hear the pounding of my heart.

I was sitting with my .458 between my knees, my thumb on the Mauser's safety catch and my forefinger along the trigger guard. However, lionesses were protected by the awful authority of a game department that was notoriously skeptical of claims of self defense and, what mattered even more, this lioness obviously had small cubs somewhere. On the other hand, we were likely well inside its critical distance, so close that if it became aware of us it would feel it had no option but to attack. I decided that if it did spot us I would whip up the rifle the moment I saw recognition dawn in its eyes and slam a 510 gr. soft-nose into it. Though I could hardly have missed, the next few seconds might well have become decidedly untidy, so I was quite relieved when several eons later it moved on.

A HUNTER REMEMBERS

At long last our male lion itself emerged from the lava flow and started to follow its females. Soren saw that it had enough mane to be a respectable trophy and told his client to take it.

At the shot the lion stumbled, recovered itself, and was gone from the field of view available to Soren and the client before they could shoot again. I stood up and saw the lion running towards us, just to our left. It was not charging, just running blind, but if it had got in amongst us the distinction might have been inconsequential. I dropped it with a .458 bullet through the chest at a range of 20 feet.

While it was being skinned later we discovered that the client had hit the lion exactly right, on the point of the shoulder, as it came towards him at an angle. He was using the European 8x68 mm with a 224-gr. RWS "Cone Point" soft-nose bullet at a muzzle velocity of 2,850 fps, a cartridge comparable to the 8mm Remington Magnum. Although they are heavily muscled beasts, it takes an uncommonly heavy lion to weigh 500 pounds. I doubt that this one went as much as 400 pounds, so the 4,000 foot-pounds of energy developed by the 8x68 should have been ample. The trouble was that the bullet blew up in the shoulder joint, smashing the bone and itself into smithereens, but penetrating no deeper. For use on dangerous game the first and most essential quality a bullet must have is the ability to reach the vitals under any circumstances and I would by far prefer to have too much penetration than not quite enough, even at the cost of less expansion.

Be that as it may, the affair ended well. We strained and grunted and heaved our lion into the safari car, and drove back to camp through herds of zebra and wildebeest concentrated by recent rains that had greened the local countryside and painted it with myriad wild flowers. The camp staff came running out as we drove in with the horn blowing to grab the client and carry him shoulder-high in an exultant lion dance.

Soon some Masai drifted in to look at the lion. The women "oohed" and "aahed" and clapped their hands in the wonder of the beast, but the warriors stood silent and aloof. They probably felt that real men used spears.

Soren's lion and the circumstances of its kill were reasonably typical — other than the failure of his client's bullet — of professionally-guided lion hunts. My own first experience with a lion was akin, but different.

One of the big cats had stampeded our cattle out of the *boma* where they were corralled at night and killed a cow a couple of hundred yards from the house. I parked my Land Rover pick-up near the carcass and, armed with the .458, waited in the back of it that night while Konde, a Masai herdsman who had hunted lions with the spear, sat in the front seat to work the headlights. The lion came at about 11:30 p.m., a pale, gray ghost that suddenly materialized beside the Land Rover. Konde switched on the lights a little too soon and the lion ran before I could get the bead of the .458 on to it. The next time it came it wasted a few seconds trying to drag the carcass away after the lights came on and I was able to get off a shot as it turned to run. It flinched at the shot, but disappeared without a sound before I could shoot again.

We came back next morning, Konde with his spear and I with a shotgun loaded with buckshot. We found a slight blood trail and followed it in a semi-circle for 100 yards into the sisal. I let Konde do the spooring while I kept my eyes swivelling alertly in all directions. Presently I smelt lion and then we found it, dead, lying behind some sisal a few paces to our right rear. It was chilling to realize that intentionally or not the lion had set up a perfect ambush and, had it still been alive, might have been upon us before we could have turned around. The .458 soft-nose had hit it just in front of the left hip and had exited some inches behind the opposite shoulder.

Although most lion trophies, whether for sport or for predator control, are bagged by baiting, there are other methods of hunting them that may sometimes be used. An acquaintance of my father's, who in the 1930s ranched what was then a wild and remote area at the junction of the Thika and Tana rivers, held that it was unfair to shoot lions in the open with a rifle. The only sporting way, he maintained, was to follow them into cover, provoke a charge and then stop them at arm's length with a shotgun. Even in the Kenya of those days he was considered to be slightly eccentric.

Actually, a 12-ga. shotgun was often used when following up a wounded lion. Sir Alfred Pease, who introduced Theodore Roosevelt to his first African lions, liked to face them in open country with his 6.5mm Mannlicher rifle in his hands and, should the rifle fail him, a cocked double-barrel shotgun on the ground between his feet for close-quarter work. Although I have not tried one on lion — I usually felt more comfortable with my familiar .458 — there is no doubt that at short range a big smoothbore has awesome stopping power. One must be very close, however. When I patterned the modified choke barrel of my 12-ga. with 00 buckshot I found that while it would still put all nine pellets into a six-inch circle at 15 yards, it spread them out over more than 12 inches at 20 yards. Consequently, I would put the maximum certain stopping range of a 12-ga. on lion at not much over 10 paces.

Before World War I, the wilder spirits among the white settlers in Kenya delighted in "galloping" lions on the Athi plains. The sport consisted of chasing lions on horseback until they turned at bay, when a charge was almost inevitable. The plan then, according to Blaney Percival in his book, *A Game Ranger's Notebook*, was to wheel the horse around and get 100 yards or so ahead of the angry cat before jumping out of the saddle to face it with rifle in hand.

Percival maintained that the horse had not been foaled that could escape a lion from a standing start within 25 yards, but that neither did the lion live that could catch a running horse.

Several men were mauled or killed while galloping lions, including one poor fellow whose saddle girth broke when his horse swerved violently to avoid a charge.

AAGAARD'S AFRICA

The most celebrated casualty was George Grey, the brother of the noted British statesman, who was killed in 1911 when he failed to stop a lion that turned on him after he had pressed it too closely. Grey leaped from his pony, fired once with the lion at 25 yards, again at five yards, and then the lion hurled him to the ground and shook him like a terrier with a mouse. Grey's companions galloped up and shot the lion off him, but he died a few days later from his injuries.

The Portuguese hunters in Mozambique used to bring in lions with a call fashioned from a gourd or large can. Although one would think that calling certainly ought to work with animals that are as social, territorial and vocal as lions are, I have not heard of the technique being used as standard procedure anywhere else in Africa. I do know of a case where a soft call imitating a lioness was used to bring in a lion who had become separated from his females and was looking for them. I have also watched Syd Downey, the dean of East African professional hunters, bring in two big maned lions on the dead run by playing a tape of hyenas squabbling over a kill, but that was in the Mara Game Reserve several years after he had retired.

Probably the most sporting method of hunting lions is to track them up. This was seldom feasible in Kenya, but it is used in Botswana in the sandy terrain of the Kalahari Desert. I am told that one usually does not catch up with the lion until it has bedded down and that it is then pushed from one patch of cover to another until it angrily refuses to be pushed any more, certainly making for interesting encounters if the hunter is afoot. I gather, however, that lions are often shot from the hunting car nowadays, quite indefensible as far as I am concerned.

It is not uncommon to be able to watch a lion making a kill in the National Parks of East Africa. To be successful the lion must normally get to within about 20 yards of its intended prey, either by stalking or by lying in ambush, often at a waterhole. Then comes a sudden rush and, before the surprised quarry can get away, the lion rears up to place one paw on its withers and

152

A HUNTER REMEMBERS

another on its neck or face, and pulls it down. As the dust clears one sees that the lion has a stranglehold on the throat, or sometimes over the nose and mouth of the victim. Smaller animals, such as baby warthogs, are generally killed by a bite through the chest. Of course, the lions are not always successful and many of their hunts end in failure.

Quite a few hunters have survived being caught by a lion. Tony Henley, who spent 20 minutes lying under a badly wounded lion before his client carefully shot it off him, thinks that most lions don't quite know how to go about tackling a creature that walks on two legs, is just a little too large for the chest-crushing technique and lacks the convenient length of neck of an antelope or zebra. While many human victims are indeed killed immediately, and man-eating lions are no doubt another matter, I believe that there may well be some substance to Henley's theory where normal lions are concerned.

"Nature fakers", as Theodore Roosevelt called them, like to claim that only vile man hunts for fun and that "natural" predators kill only when they are hungry. This is a thorough-going fallacy. Lions, like domestic housecats, often kill for sport.

One wet afternoon Berit and I took the kids for a drive in the Nairobi National Park. Not five miles from the Hilton Hotel tower in downtown Nairobi we came on a couple of lionesses beside a freshly killed wildebeest. After waiting a while in vain for them to start feeding, we drove on in search of the rest of the pride. Half a mile farther on we found a small pride, six or seven lionesses and juveniles but without any mature males, lying below a little ridge, in the rain. The group looked just as thoroughly miserable as any wet cats can be.

Suddenly a herd of wildebeest came galloping along the ridge above the lions. What they were running from or where they were going we could not tell. Most likely the *gnus* themselves did not know. Instantly the lions threw off their lethargy, staring, with quickening interest, at the passing wildebeest. A big lioness sprang to its feet and started running along the foot

153

of the ridge and the rest followed. They got in front of the wildebeest, and cut up the ridge and over the crest to intercept them. There was a mad melee as the startled antelope jinked and ran in every direction, then we saw that the big lioness had a kicking wildebeest calf by the throat.

Soon the calf went limp, and the lioness dropped it and stood panting. Whereupon the victim revived, scrambled to its feet and, with an outraged bellow, promptly charged the lioness, who lept aside in surprise. For a few seconds the lions stood as if nonplussed while the little wildebeest shook its head belligerently at them. Then they closed in on it. One caught it by the muzzle, another by a hind leg and they pulled in different directions. They played with it as a cat plays with a mouse for several minutes, until at last one of the lionesses took a proper stranglehold and finished the job. Then, without making any attempt to feed, the lions sauntered off, leaving the carcass to the vultures. When we returned to the first kill we found that it, too, had been abandoned.

A quick visit to an African national park all too often leaves a tourist with a one-sided and Disneyesque impression of lions. He encounters them flopped out in the shade of a tree, the big black-maned fellow asleep on its back with all four paws in the air and a cub playing with the twitching tuft of its tail, while two lionesses rub faces and lick each other affectionately. Seeing them thus, lady tourists used to irritate my wife by declaring that they were just like their darling little tabby-cats back home. How ridiculous, Berit thought, to compare a silly, spoilt, pink-bowed house pet to our magnificent wild lions. But years later I brought home two small kittens that someone had dumped out on a county road to starve and we learned that the tourist ladies were quite right. Domestic cats do move, and play, and greet each other, and flop down, and stalk, and pounce, just like lions.

Nevertheless, lions are not just overgrown house pets. They are large, powerful, ruthless predators that kill for a living.

A HUNTER REMEMBERS

Where they are hunted, lions have generally learned to avoid all contact with humans. In national parks, though, where they have been protected for several generations, lions have no reason to regard man as other than an upright meal and they can be exceedingly dangerous.

There exists a rumor about a Volkswagen tourist bus that got hopelessly stuck in a *kargona* (dry wash) in the Serengeti National Park some years ago. The driver and an unarmed national parks guide decided to walk out a mile or so to the main road to get help, but they never reached it. Lions are supposed to have caught and eaten them both. The story is probably apocryphal, but it certainly could have happened, particularly had the pair panicked and tried to run.

John Kingsley-Heath, a well-known professional hunter from Kenya who later moved to Botswana and established Safari South as one of Africa's leading hunting operations and who has himself survived an intimate encounter with a vexed lion, put matters in their proper perspective quite succinctly when a radio talk-show host asked him how lions regarded people.

"It is my opinion," John replied, "that lions regard humans as being nothing more than mobile hamburgers !"

There is no sound, not even the crazy cackling of the hyena, that is more evocative of Africa than a lion calling in the night.

"Whose land is this ? MINE...Mine...mine...mine."

15

Rhino

Sportsmen, writing of African adventures as far back as the turn of the 20th century prophesied, to a man, the decline and eventual extinction of rhinoceros. Sadly, events have proven their dire prediction correct. Rhinos, the Indian, Javan and Sumatran species, and the white and black varieties native to Africa, are very much in danger of disappearing from the face of this earth. And man has been the cause of it, even if not in the precise manner of the prognosticators of nine decades ago. Poachers have done it, along with creeping civilization that denies habitat to all species that are farther down the food chain than is man. Mainly, it's been poachers, though, operating in numbers and with arms that the most far-seeing conservationist of yore could not have imagined. Only in the Republic of South Africa, where game department officials have the sanction and the equipment to treat poachers like the lawless murderers that they are, is the rhino relatively — and only relatively — safe.

But it wasn't always like that. Thirty years ago, or a bit more, rhinos in Kenya were plentiful to the point of being a nuisance, and they were control-hunted along with many other species. Licenses could, in some circumstances, be inexpensive and easy to obtain. That's how my brother-in-law, Pete Davey, and Joe Cheffings, and I happened to be in John Hunter's Marukeni

157

AAGAARD'S AFRICA

District with permits for a pair of the beasts. Hunter, you see, had been ordered to shoot 1000 rhino to enable Kamba tribesmen to settle there.

Even when that had been done, the government still thought that there were too many rhino, and therefore issued a number of licenses to hunters at reduced price. However, they were still expensive enough that we would have to sell the rhino horns to help cover the costs, so Pete and I agreed to pool our resources, buy two licenses and hunt together. Joe decided to come along for the ride, and to help with chores.

When we eventually found a suitable rhino Pete had his .458 and I a .375 H & H. Joe, being without a rhino license, had been charged with provision of meat for the camp, and was carrying Pete's trusty little 7 mm Brno.

Pete began the festivities by belting the rhino in the shoulder area, and I fired immediately after him. Unfortunately I was standing to one side of Pete and a little behind him, and the muzzle blast from my .375 knocked his hat off and painfully, if temporarily, deafened him.

It's odd how events can change priorities. Here we were, three grown men surrounded by a wounded and dangerous rhinoceros, and Pete stopped the proceedings for long enough to let me know how little he thought of my selection of a place from which to shoot — as I recollect most of what he said consisted of four-letter words. The rhino, meanwhile, went into a spin, turning round and around in the dust, until Pete and I had had our talk. Then Pete gave it a second .458, in the center of the chest, and I added another .375 in the shoulder. The rhino's response to all this was to turn away from us as if to leave. And that's when Joe Cheffings stuck a 175-gr., 7mm soft-nose into its rear end and brought it down. He claimed that it was perfectly obvious; he had killed the rhino while all our thunder failed to do so, and with a 7x57 mm, into the bargain.

In those days, as noted earlier, rhinos were common. They swarmed across Voi and the Tsavo country. The Mara Game

158

A HUNTER REMEMBERS

Reserve and the Mountain National Parks, were almost overcrowded with them. "Gertie", "Gladys" and the rest of their marvelously long-horned kin thrilled the tourists at wondrous Amboseli in those days, and rhinos ofttimes disputed possession of the waterhole with the elephants at fabulous Treetops.

Even in the hunting areas they were in such numbers that we tended to regard them as being rather a nuisance. Anywhere in the bush country, or in the forests, or wherever there was suitable cover outside of the settled areas one could expect to find rhino paths and to note their round, dessert-plate diameter tracks that showed three distinct toes. (Hippo, by the way, have four toes.) On hard ground three ellipses from the toe nails might be all that was discernable, or perhaps just one, but that was sufficient identification. So too were the scrapes where they deposited their grape fruit-size droppings before kicking and scratching them around with their hind feet, at the same time often raking nearby vegetation with their horns. The Africans say that rhinos do this because their lords, the elephants, do not like to see droppings resembling their own lying about.

The droppings of both black rhino and elephants contain nothing much but the fibrous remnants of twigs and bark, and are quite inoffensive. When Jan and Lasse Allan were running a tented camp for tourists at "Tsavo Tsafaris" Lasse had a brilliant bed of the most glorious zinnias outside their home. In response to queries as to how she could get them to grow so well in that thin and barren soil, she would merely point to the abundant droppings on a nearby elephant and rhino highway that led down to the river.

Every self-respecting rhino had a retinue of red- or yellow-billed tickbirds, which are related to starlings. They not only attended to its external parasites, but even more important gave it air cover and early warning of approaching danger. Their high-pitched chittering as they flew up in alarm (a sound I have been too deaf to hear for many years, which was a real handicap, believe me) was often the first intimation one had of a rhino's

159

nearby presence, though they did attend on buffalo, eland and giraffe as well. Then there might sound a series of sharp snorts, rather like a steam locomotive laboring to haul the Uganda Mail up the grade out of the Great Rift Valley, and, "Oh my Gawd, here comes trouble again!"

Joe Cheffings and I were exploring a rocky knoll looking for a place to hang a leopard bait when trouble developed, and in exactly that sequence. First came the flight of tickbirds, then the puffing of *two* of nature's answer to a steam engine, then a pair of rhino appeared out of the scrub, come to dispute our right to their turf. Joe, seeking to dissuade the animals, fired a shot into the air and then, anticipating the failure of his ploy, stepped back to clear a path for them. As he did so, he slipped on a loose stone, and fell flat on his back. Almost simultaneously I put a shot into the ground in front of them, tried to leap aside, slipped and fell on my back also. The sight of two lunatic humans lying on the ground, yelling and waving their legs in the air so disconcerted the rhinos that rather than run over the top of us they split and passed one to each side, puffing furiously in confused amazement. The last we saw of them, one of the pair crossed a ridge a good mile away, still trotting along at a cracking pace.

The main problem in dealing with rhinos in colonial Kenya, was that they were strictly protected, and the game department was not very sympathetic to claims of self defense. Had Joe or I actually shot one of those two animals, and then failed to prove that it was a "last-ditch" act, we would certainly have lost our "Assistant's Permits" and might have lost a good measure of personal freedom as well. The chief game wardens of those days did not hesitate to hold hunters accountable for their actions and the penalties for failing to conduct oneself responsibly were severe. Joe and I, and Fritz Walter, had already been through one such inquisition and the memory of those proceedings was enough that we worked very hard to avoid actually having to shoot a rhinoceros.

A HUNTER REMEMBERS

Well, almost.... Once, many years ago, Joe went buffalo hunting near the Seven Forks of the Tana River, accompanied by his newly wedded wife, Simonne. They found a herd, and Joe hammered a bull, but it did not drop immediately. As he started to follow it up, with Simonne a little way behind him, a rhino appeared on their flank, coming on at a hard trot. Joe stepped smartly behind a tree, but then saw that the rhino was heading directly for Simonne, who was caught out in the open.

Since coming to Kenya, at the age of 17, Joe had itched to bag a rhino, and here was an excuse of sorts. Besides, he really had grown quite fond of Simonne, so he stepped out and shot the rhino, which went into a spin and fell down.

He was already starting to formulate the justification he would have to present to the game department, when to his immense relief he found a poisoned arrow sticking in the animal's side, with the wound still fresh and bleeding. Obviously, it had been running from a Kamba bowman who must have plinked it only a few minutes previously. That put a very different aspect on the matter. It was no longer a dubious case of self defense. Instead, Joe had virtuously and as in duty bound finished off a wounded, dangerous animal that might otherwise have terrorized the district and spitted who knows how many innocent bush dwellers.

Joe never wanted to shoot another rhino, and as I had taken the only one I will ever willingly kill, thereafter we did indeed take all necessary evasive action upon encountering them.

Evasive action is often appropriate. A rhino is not a wantonly cruel animal; merely an impolite one. Neither is it accustomed to any back-talk from its neighbors. The man or beast who invades a rhino's space is going to be invited — rather pointedly — to leave. If a rhino wants to go somewhere, it goes there by what it considers to be the best route; and Heaven help him who *stays* in a rhino's path.

In that regard, it is truly amazing how fast a fellow can scramble up a totally unclimable, thorn-bedecked tree when

161

there is an irate rhino snorting at his heels. Lacking a tree — thorny or not — when a rhino charges blindy at a sound or at a whiff of scent, it is sometimes possible to get out of trouble by running around downwind of the behemoth, so that it loses track of *why* it is charging and just goes steaming off in the last direction in which it was pointed.

Sometimes one could often stop a rhino by shouting at it, or by putting a shot in the ground right under its nose. In the national parks with a Land Rover full of camera tourists we would on occasion provoke a charge, and let the animal come right in while the cameras whirred and the clients gasped. At the last second we would turn the rhino by vigorously slapping the outside of the door, and shouting loudly. The technique was almost, but not quite, infallible.

Joe usually had a rhino dent or two somewhere on his truck, and one that refused to stop for Soren Lindstrom swept its horn up along his door, neatly hooked his watch band, and tore it off his wrist.

Although most charges may be mere demonstrations, every now and again one will come on in dead earnest, meaning every bit of it.

A Swedish friend of mine named Gunnar Lundstam, accompanied by an unarmed companion, was hunting waterbuck along the Athi River in Block 29, and was carrying a .308 Winchester rifle with 150-gr. soft-point bullets. After working his way slowly and painfully through a belt of dense thorn brush, Gunnar broke out into a sort of bay on the far side, some distance in front of his companion. He immediately became aware of a rhino in the more open country ahead, as it had obviously heard or scented them and was already launched in a full-out charge.

Boxed in as he was by the wait-a-bit thorn, Gunnar could not run in any direction, and there were no trees. So he shouted at the rhino, telling it somewhat abusively to go away. It paid not the slightest attention. Then he put a shot in the ground in front of it. A cloud of dust and sand spurted up right in its face. Surely that must turn it, thought Gunnar. But no, without faltering the rhino kept coming determinedly straight at him, as if locked on by radar. Gunnar realized that he would have to try to shoot it.

Now, even with a suitable heavy rifle, an onrushing rhino presents something of a problem. Its horns tend to shield its brain, while its lowered snout covers most of its chest, which is, in any case, often obscured by brush or high grass. With a large caliber "solid" bullet one can try to break a shoulder, causing the beast to swerve to that side, but Gunnar doubted that his little soft-point was up to the job. Instead he tried for the spine at the withers, holding just over the top of the horn.

To his dismay the rhino did not even flinch. It was now upon him, and as there was no time for another shot all he could do was to dodge desperately aside at the last possible moment. Perhaps he left it too late. The rhino swung its head in passing. Its horn raked up along Gunnar's chest, breaking some ribs, then ripped open the front of his neck and smashed his lower jaw. He was flung to the ground, almost unconscious. He vaguely remembers that the rhino spun around and stood over him for several moments, but he lay still and presently it went away.

Gunnar was bleeding like a stuck pig from the wound in his neck. His companion tied the tattered remnants of Gunnar's shirt around it, and then half led and half carried him the two miles out to the truck. By the greatest of good fortune Gunnar's wife, who happened to be a registered nurse, was in camp. She was able to bring the bleeding somewhat under control before driving him post-haste to the village of Mitito Andei, whence a telephone call to the Flying Doctor Service brought an airplane to carry him to the hospital in Nairobi.

Gunnar worked for a quasi-government outfit that gave him two weeks sick leave after he got out of the hospital. He spent most of it in one of the better hunting blocks in Masailand, where he got himself well and truly charged by a buffalo. This time, however, he was properly armed with a .458 and managed to stop the bull before it reached him. Thereafter he never went afield without a first aid kit containing several military-style field dressings on his belt, and was seldom seen with any rifle smaller than a .375 H & H in his hands.

But, in truth, most rhino encounters were not very serious, and they were ofttimes quite hilarious. One I will never forget involved a pal I'll call Mike, who went into a thicket carrying a roll of toilet paper. Suddenly we heard a commotion and a loud yell. A shocked and outraged rhino rushed out the far side of the covert, while a thoroughly frightened and embarrassed Mike came running out our end of it clutching the toilet paper in one hand and holding up his pants with the other.

Surprisingly enough, rhino are easily tamed, after which they usually become very docile. The well-known animal trapper Carr-Hartley had a couple on his property near Rumuruti that could be ridden bare-backed by little children, and one that had been in captivity less than a week delighted in having people scratch it under the chin. In contrast a young buffalo bull in the next pen backed into the far corner and glared in irascible resentment at anyone who approached it. There is a delightful, and possibly apocryphal, story of a trapper who caught a rhino by building a stockade and baiting it with salt. Then he could find no buyer, so after several weeks of cutting and hauling brush to feed the beast, he decided to turn it loose. But when the gate was opened the rhino stuck its head out, took one look at the cruel and disorderly world outside, and dashed back into the security of the stockade. It knew where it had it good.

The only rhino that has been native to Kenya in historical times is the so-called black rhinoceros, *Diceros bicornis*. A mature adult stands about five feet high at the shoulder, and weighs around 2,500 pounds. They are browsers and have a pointed, prehensile upper lip with which they are quite adept at stripping leaves and twigs from thorny vegetation. Their hide is practically hairless; they love to wallow and luxuriate in dust baths. Consequently, together with elephants, warthogs and to some extent buffalo, they tend to take on the color of the soil.

The other African rhino is the white (or square-lipped) rhinoceros, *Ceratotherium simus simus*, that inhabits two widely separated areas, one in South Africa and the other to the west of the Nile in northern central Africa. I have encountered only the northern race of this species, and then only in the Murchison Falls National Park in Uganda, where it had been introduced. The great beasts grazed placidly on the coarse grasses and did not even bother to raise their heads as we drove in among them. They are of a different shape than the black rhino, particularly as regards their heads, have an peculiar hump on their necks, and are much larger, weighing perhaps twice as much. They are essentially grazers, and are no more white in color than the black rhino is black.

How the northern white rhino has fared through the revolutions, blatant poaching and rampaging armies that have ravaged the countries in its range in recent years is unknown, but it is undoubtedly very close to extinction. In contrast the southern race has been so well managed by the South African government that a certain number of excess animals can be made available to trophy collectors, or for export as stockers to other countries. For a time there was a promising nucleus of half-a-dozen of South African white rhino in the Meru National Park in Kenya, but despite being watched over by an armed guard all were slaughtered by poachers.

The black rhinoceros has gone from being a relatively common animal to near extinction in scant decades. The cause is wholesale poaching, brought on by a dramatic increase in the price of rhino horn. As if the poor, bumbling, myopic beast did not already have sufficient trouble trying to cope with encroaching civilization, the market value of the curious, fibrous, agglutinated hair-like growths on its snout shot up from perhaps $60 a pound to somewhere around $600 - $700 a pound.

Perhaps, however, the rhino has a chance. Man, the species

that hunts every other species on earth, has also demonstrated the willingness to do what is needed to preserve other species; though sometimes the process takes a while to get started. In that respect, governments have begun to equip their game departments to handle poachers and to negotiate treaties to remove the market influence. It has worked with whales and leopards, and even alligators, and maybe it will work with rhinos, too.

I hope so, for the rhino is an integral part of Africa's landscape and the place just wouldn't be the same without it.

16

Happy Safari

Leonard S. Burke, a tall, dark chap from Houston, Texas, had a delightfully warm, friendly grin on his face when we met him at the airport and to the best of my recollection he stopped smiling during the next three weeks only in order to laugh. He was on holiday in Africa and by gosh, he was going to enjoy himself. Petite Connie Burke who, make no mistake, possesses a core of steel, was equally friendly and smiling. The augurers promised a good safari.

Because Connie did not hunt (at least, not then), Berit, who was seven months pregnant, left our first-born, Erik, with his grandmother and came along to keep her company. We camped in a grove of tall, wide-spreading, yellow-barked acacia trees close to the southern Uaso Nyiro River in Masailand, a spot from which we could hunt both the Loita Plains and the more wooded country above Narok. It was beautiful country that, due to its 6,000-foot elevation and constant breeze, had an entirely delightful climate. During the Burkes' stay the temperature never got over 80° F, not even on the hottest day, and the evenings were cool enough that a jacket by the campfire and two or three blankets on the bed felt good. The hyenas whooped madly — that most African of sounds — and not uncommonly one awoke to a lion's hoarse rumbling in the night.

AAGAARD'S AFRICA

Prior to this, his first safari, Len Burke had never hunted anything larger than a rabbit. But he had persuaded a knowledgeable friend to coach him in rifle shooting and had practiced a good deal at the range before he came. We had hired a Winchester .30-'06 for him and he shot it very nicely when we checked its zero the first afternoon in camp. He also proved that he could adequately manage my scope-sighted .375, which he was going to use for dangerous game. Besides that, he seemed willing to listen and to do as he was told.

The first morning we stalked a group of zebra on the Loita Plains until we had a clear shot at a small, black-striped stallion. Kinuno put up the crossed shooting sticks to help support the rifle and we clearly heard the bullet strike. The stallion broke into a dead run, however, so I sat down with the .375 and got another bullet into it, rather far back through a kidney. As it turned out it was not needed because Len's shot had been in the lungs, but he had a horror of losing wounded game and, to my delight, asked me to collaborate if I thought it necessary.

Berit, Kinuno and I had the zebra skinned in short order, and we put most of the meat in the Toyota as well, to use as leopard bait. Then, after a cup of tea and cookies from the chuck box, we wandered on over the rolling, grassy, plains until we spotted a herd of Grant's gazelle feeding in a patch of whistling thorn. Whistling thorn is actually a low, scrubby acacia that bears a profusion of round galls about the size of walnuts, in which live colonies of pugnacious ants that swarm out to defend their host whenever the bush is disturbed, a perfect example of symbiosis. When the wind blows across the ants' entrance holes in the galls, a wavering, mournful whistle may be heard. In any case, the thorn brush would offer some cover for an approach and, since there were several large bucks with the gazelles, we left the vehicle and made our stalk.

Granti are among the largest of the true gazelles, with a mature buck weighing 150-175 pounds and I think the handsomest of them all. The light fawn of their coats contrasts

A HUNTER REMEMBERS

with their white bellies, black outlined white rump patches, and chestnut and black streaked faces, while their long, strongly-ringed, flared horns sweep to an impressive height above their neat, short-muzzled heads. Eventually we reached a point about 150 paces from the bunch and, after some maneuvering, got a clear shot at what I had judged was the biggest buck. This time no collaboration was needed, as Len drilled it precisely through the center of the shoulder area.

The next few days we continued to hunt the so-called "plains game", collecting wildebeest, Thomson's gazelle and a second zebra, and also hung leopard baits. While looking for a suitable tree in which to place a bait we happened on a very big impala and went after it, leaving Connie and Berit in the Toyota. It led us in circles, and presently the ladies watched Kinuno and me cross an open aisle in the brush with Len following close behind. Suddenly he froze, and then started dancing about and slapping at himself. He hurriedly unbuckled his belt and tore his trousers off and frenziedly tried to brush something off his long legs. He had stepped into a column of safari (or driver) ants and, quite literally, had ants in his pants. That finished the impala hunt. The ladies were still giggling when we got back to the vehicle.

Some days later we had a customer on one of the baits. We built a blind 30 yards from it in a clump of brush, with a solid support for the rifle in front of the shooting hole. While Kinuno, whose dark face would be less likely to be spotted, kept watch, Len and I lay back, each with a book, to wait. The minutes dragged by while the sun slowly sank towards the horizon, until Kinuno suddenly grasped my knee. There was a leopard on the feeding branch, glowing black and gold where the dying sun illuminated it. It looked small and somehow feminine.

"M'ke?" I breathed into Kinuno's ear.

He nodded agreement that it was a female. It was legal to take females, but we by all means avoided doing so. It would have been a horrible tragedy to shoot a female find she was in milk and realize that one had left a litter of cubs to starve. Len was

171

staring inquiringly at us. I pointed towards the shooting hole and whispered, "Female, take a look, but do not shoot."

As we watched the leopard looked down and gave a strange, soft call. The brush at the foot of the tree stirred and a half-grown cub scrambled up to join its mother. We stayed until black night, and the next day we replenished the bait so that Connie and Berit could watch the show. But when a couple of evenings later we sent the camp staff to see them, the leopards did not come. It turned out that the carnivorous safari ants had found the bait and were swarming so aggressively over it that the leopards had surrendered it.

A constant stream of Masai visited the camp to look at the white people and be amused by their strange and utterly incomprehensible ways and customs. They would seat themselves hopefully by the kitchen fire and presently Nzioka the cook would offer them a cup of hot, sweet, milky tea, as was only proper (he did limit them to one cup each per day, though). Nzioka had a gift for languages, he spoke some Swedish and Italian through having worked for families of those nationalities and could get along quite well in Masai, although it was as different from his native Kikamba as Russian is from English. One day he asked us whether the *wageni* (foreign guests) would be interested in photographing two Masai women? For five shillings each they would come back next day and pose dressed in all their finery. The bargain was struck and the two ladies showed up decked out in beaded leather petticoats with ocher-dyed cotton *shukas* knotted over the right shoulder and surmounted by patterned cotton shawls. They wore wide, beaded belts, beaded ear ornaments and around their necks overlapping tiers of beaded collars from which long strings of bright beads dangled down to their knees. Around their wrists and ankles brass bangles gleamed against the dark skin and the younger, a cheerful, smiling lass, carried a beaded and decorated gourd of curdled milk. The gourds are rinsed out with cow urine and smoked before the milk is allowed to stand in them to curdle, which gives it a characteristic flavor. If one can overlook the odd dead fly it is very good, refreshing stuff. "Karamoja" Bell swore by it, saying that, together with smoked elephant meat, it formed the perfect diet for an elephant hunter.

Both the women were equally as pregnant as Berit. They gently patted her stomach in approval and insisted that the three of them should be photographed together. Berit stood with her hands behind her back, but that would not do at all. They took her hands and showed her that she should clasp them demurely in front of her, as if everyone ought to know that was the only way for a lady to pose.

Peter Davey brought a friend of Len's down for a couple of days. Ron worked for an airline and happened to be in Kenya on a short trip. While Len and I were beating the brush for a bushbuck or some such, Pete and Kinuno took Ron out to see if they could get him a Thomson's gazelle. They chased a likely specimen all over the wide-open plains and finally Ron crippled it. Pete took a shot at it with my .375 and missed. The little gazelle (they weigh perhaps 60 pounds on the hoof) was running directly away and the range was increasing every second. Pete passed the rifle to Kinuno and told him to try. Kinuno sat down, rested the fore-end on the shooting sticks, grimaced in concentration and shot the gazelle perfectly through the heart from the tail end. So much for the great white hunters!

Len and I got our bushbuck, a smallish one, and spent a whole morning trying to get a shot at a very handsome 27-inch impala. It lived at the edge of the brush surrounding a large open plain. We tried to approach it by the easy and obvious route, but every time we got nearly in range something went wrong, the wind gave us away or we ran out of cover and were spotted. Pretty soon if we kept disturbing it the buck would move out altogether, so we backed off, made a big circle that took us about an hour to complete, and crawled up on the impala from a totally different and unexpected direction. That worked, and Len made the most of a broadside opportunity at

226 long paces by hitting it through the center of the chest directly above the foreleg, the perfect spot in which to place a vital shot.

I reckoned he was ready for buffalo, so dawn one morning saw us hunting along the edge of the 500-foot deep gorge of the Siapei River. Buffalo herds often grazed the river flats way below. We saw none this day, but around mid-morning we found a lone buffalo bull on a bench about halfway down. As we watched, it ambled into a patch of shady trees and brush probably to bed down until the cool of evening. We went back half a mile, scrambled down to the bench and carefully stalked the mott of brush. Skirting around it, tense and adrenalin-charged, we peered hopefully into the cool, dense black shade. Kinuno caught a swish of its tail and pointed. Gradually we made out the black form and decided which end was which.

I nudged Len, "Shoot!"

With the 2½ X scope Len had no trouble seeing where to hold. At his shot the bull turned and lurched away deeper into the thicket. I tried to get a .458 bullet into it, but through my iron sights it was indistinguishable from the dark shadows and I did not do much good. Fortunately, Len had hit it passably well and some minutes later we were relieved to hear its sad death bellows. The toughest part was getting the head, the cape and as much of the meat as we could manage back up the sheer wall of the gorge.

Then we went bird hunting. Len, who enjoyed the shotgun, spent an afternoon with the doves and the flighting green and olive pigeons, while Berit bird-dogged for him. That evening he marinated the breasts in a sauce that he and Nzioka concocted and broiled them on a grill over the embers of an acacia-wood fire — superb! It was decided that Connie should try to bag a few of the numerous guinea fowl. I don't think she had ever pulled a trigger before. We found a large flock of guineas busily engaged in scratching around in the dust. A convenient big bush provided cover. I put Kinuno in the lead, with Connie and the

A HUNTER REMEMBERS

shotgun close behind, and the rest of us tagging along after. Kinuno crouched down and stalked the guineas as if they were record book kudu, dead serious. When they reached the bush he took Connie's arm and pointed out the unsuspecting fowl.

"*Piga,*" he said, and stuck his fingers in his ears.

Connie raised the shotgun, closed her eyes, and pulled both triggers, *blam-blam!* Kinuno watched disconsolately as the startled flock thundered into the air, leaving no victims behind, and then turned around with a shocked expression as the rest of us started laughing. But when he saw that even Len was doubled up with glee, a broad grin slowly split his stolid face.

We packed up the camp and moved most of the way across Kenya to Block 21A on the Galana River the hot, low, semi-arid brush country between Tsavo Park and the coast. We spent a night in Nairobi on the way and Berit collected young Erik, who perforce had to come with us. So we rolled down the Mombasa road en route to elephant country with a baby's crib lashed to the roof of the hunting car. We camped in a no-hunting sanctuary that ran a mile deep along the river, close to a game trail that led to a watering place. One evening a bunch of elephant that had come to drink stampeded, perhaps they had suddenly caught our scent, or heard pots clattering in the kitchen. In their panic-stricken flight they knocked over a latrine tent, which luckily was unoccupied at the time.

Len added a warthog to his collection and an old lesser kudu with an inch or two worn off the tips of its horns. We found a herd of fringe-eared oryx, the big, hardy desert antelopes with javelin-like horns that Sir Winston Churchill described as resembling a troop of lancers, up near the Kulalu Hills on the Tsavo border. Len took a very fine, heavy-horned 29½-inch bull out of the bunch and was delighted. So were we and the camp staff because, unexpectedly, oryx make very fine eating.

The Galana was not reckoned to be good buffalo country, for the horns of animals from that area tend to be small and ugly. But one day we came across some bachelor bulls feeding along a brushy draw and were surprised to notice that one of them had a very fine, massive head, much better than Len's first one. We got in front of them and let them come to us. After a little excitement Len collected the big one.

But for the most part we hunted elephant. They crossed back and forth from Tsavo Park and knew exactly where the boundary lay. If one bashed a bull anywhere near the boundary, it would by all means endeavor to get across it. If it succeeded, if it fell even one yard across the line, it became the property of the National Parks and the hunter had lost his trophy, but was nevertheless considered to have filled his license. After looking over many jumbos and finding only cows, calves and young bulls with mere cigarettes sticking out of their mouths, we at last chanced on two bulls travelling together and safely many miles from the boundary. One was obviously immature, but the other bore long, slender, evenly-curved tusks. I told Len that they would not go over 60 pounds, each side, but that with their length they would make a beautiful trophy.

"Fine," he replied, "let's go get him."

They were just loafing along, but even then an elephant can cover an amazing amount of ground in short order, and we had to hustle to catch up with them, while taking advantage of the wind and of a little cover as we got closer. Eventually, Len had a clear heart/lung shot at perhaps 60 yards, but did not make enough allowance for its pace and got it a touch far back and a little low. As it turned away I tried unsuccessfully for the spine above the root of the tail. Kinuno and I ran after it and pounded its rear end further and at last it went down.

As we walked up to it, the elephant shrank and the closer we got to it the smaller it became, which is the opposite of the normal phenomenon. Usually, when an elephant is lying on its side one cannot see over its belly, but the top of the belly of this one came barely chest-high. The darn-fool thing was a dwarf! Instead of weighing 60 pounds a side, the tusks went barely 40 pounds each, though they measured 6½ feet in length. What had fooled us, I believe, was that there had been no other adult elephant with it to give us a scale of its size. I was thoroughly abashed at having misjudged an animal so badly, but Len made light of it. It was his elephant, he said, and he was happy with it. Besides, the small tusks would fit perfectly in their low-ceilinged apartment. Spoken like a gentleman and a true sportsman.

We fetched the crew from camp to chop out the ivory, remove the feet and take the ears for leather. We left them a pickup and a rifle, and drove away to look at the country, identify some birds, chase the giraffe, take a few pictures and savor the last day of the safari.

While they were busy at their work the crew was startled by a loud shriek and looked up to see two cow elephants charging down on them, trumpeting and screaming in outrage. Kinuno responded to the threat by grabbing up a rifle and firing a shot in the air. Kamonde, a Kamba tribesman whom I had hired, temporarily at least, away from my sister, Grete, started the vehicle and tried to drive off. And Mutunga, a young relative of Kamonde's that Berit hired for camp staff, dove headlong into the back of the truck and hid under an elephant ear that was lying there. The commotion was more than either of the cows was willing to endure, and the pair swerved aside and went away, still crying murder, which from their point of view it was.

Len and Connie became so enamored of Africa that they came back many times to hunt on different parts of the continent. Eventually Connie, too, took up the rifle and became a very experienced huntress. Five years later, when Len brought Ronnie Berman to hunt with me, the wheel had turned almost full circle. Len had all the African trophies he wanted, save one, and now found it more satisfying to watch his young protege begin to experience it and to fall in love with it all, rather than to try do it all over again himself. He fired only one shot on the whole trip, to collect the gerenuk he had regretted not buying a license for on that first, wonderful, memorable, happy safari.

17

Barsalinga
Buffalo

You can't take it with you, they say. Eventually comes the realization that trophies, of themselves, have little meaning, and that having one's name listed in a book does not mean much, either. Only the memories are of enduring value.

What goes into the making of a memorable hunt? There are many possible ingredients. Success in the sense of bagging the sought-after quarry may not be an absolute essential, but it adds a certain savor. The bonds forged between companions engaged in a joint enterprise are important. There is great satisfaction to be had from testing one's skills, endurance, courage and self-discipline, and passing the test. Being happy with the outcome — the knowing that "it was done right" — means a lot. So does feeling the sense of adventure, of exploring new and exciting country, and of returning to the wilderness to play man's original role in it. These things are the essentials. The mere killing of an animal, even if it is a new world record, is nothing. The things that go into hunting are what matter.

When I first saw it in the mid-1950s, Isiolo, Kenya's "Gateway to the Northern Frontier", was a fascinating little town. Its dusty streets thronged with a fantastic variety of people from many different tribes and conditions of life. Elephants came to eat the petunias in the District Commissioner's garden and had to be shot, leading to a sharp quarrel between the commissioner's staff and Game Department officials as to who was responsible for disposing of the remains. The Game Department won that skirmish handily when, after a few days, an unmistakable effluvium started to waft gently through the windows of the D.C.'s bungalow...or so legend has it.

Joe Cheffings, Fritz Walter and I arrived in Isiolo one afternoon, having driven up in my old short wheelbase Land Rover and Joe's VW "Beetle". As was customary, we called on the Game Warden to let him know we would be in his area and to ask advice. George Adamson was out on safari, but we talked with his wife Joy, who had not yet achieved fame with her book *Born Free*, about the lioness Elsa. Then after packing all our chattels in the Land Rover and obtaining our permits to enter a closed district from Dermie O'Shea, the District Officer, with whom we left the VW, we set out to look for buffalo around Barsalinga on the Northern Uaso Nyiro. (*Uaso* means river, and *nyiro* can be translated as dark or muddy.)

We traveled light in those days, but even so the little Land Rover was well laden and rather cramped for space with five men aboard, as Joe had brought along a couple of employees from the coffee plantation he managed. Since all this country is inhabited, though thinly, we needed someone to look after our camp while we were gone, and one man would have been lonely and easily intimidated by the wild, spear-toting local gentry.

It was only some 60 miles to Barsalinga, but the road was nothing more than a rutted track that threaded its way over low, barren hills sparsely clad with thorn brush and along *luggas* (dry stream beds) lined with scrabbly little acacia trees. It was so rough that it permitted a maximum average speed of about 10 m.p.h. and we had to spend a night on the way. Fritz shot a gerenuk (giraffe-necked gazelle) for meat — it did have rather good horns, too — and we threw our sleeping bags down on the stony hillside beside the Land Rover. In this dry, semi-desert country it became almost chilly as soon as the sun went down.

Next morning we crossed the Kipsing Lugga, where the sand was still damp and water was obtainable by digging, and eventually came to a bore-hole (well) that the benevolent Government had drilled for the benefit of the people and their livestock. When we questioned the Somali tribesman who was in charge of it, he pointed to a distant conical hill and suggested we try there first. If we found nothing we should continue down to the river and hunt upstream towards a distinctive hill that had a rectangular rock balanced on its summit.

"Hawesi kosa!" he said, declaring that we could not fail to find buffalo there.

There was nothing around the conical hill but a huge flock of electric-blue vulturine guinea fowl, whose long, white-spotted neck feathers are in demand for tying salmon flies and whose name reflects their bare heads, not their habits. They make very good eating. As we had no scatter-gun or .22 rimfire with us, I chased after them with an old Smith & Wesson revolver chambered for the .38 S & W cartridge that was the British standard during World War II. I had burned up a lot of ammunition to no effect when a great martial eagle stooped down and nailed one of the scurrying guineas with contemptuous ease. But he laughs best who laughs last and, as the eagle was struggling to become airborne with its booty, I charged in shouting and waving my arms, drove it off and appropriated its prey. Well, even lions are known to scavenge from hyenas, aren't they?

We came to the river about midday. It is a shallow little stream set about with doum palms and the great wild fig trees with their wide-spreading branches, and could count as a river only in this desiccated country, where any flowing water is a miracle. We made camp by heaving a few boxes of groceries out of the Land Rover, setting up our camp cots (we had already gotten that soft) under a shady tree and lighting a fire to make tea. We took the doors off the Land Rover and set them on stakes driven into the earth to form our table and placed its seat cushions on the ground as chairs.

Presently a bunch of cattle came down to water. One of the Turkhana herdsmen told us that he had noticed a group of buffalo bedded down in a thicket close by, and offered to lead us to them. We picked up our rifles and were ready. Fritz, who was to have first shot, had a bolt-action Rigby chambered for the .400/.350, an obsolescent cartridge that drove a .35 caliber bullet weighing 310 grains at some 2,000 fps. That may not sound like much, but that long, heavy bullet penetrated forever and was a very reliable killer. Joe carried a German-made .500/.450 Nitro Express double, cartridges for which were, even then, out of production, while I had borrowed a Cogswell & Harrison bolt-action, .375 H & H to supplement my 8x60 mm Mauser.

The wind was such that we could approach to within 100 yards of the thicket using a dry draw for cover. The buffalo were still there. We saw a tail swish and then the curve of a horn as one of the animals irritably flung its head about. The herdsman and I remained in the draw while Joe and Fritz crawled in as close as the indifferent cover permitted. They could not get a clear shot and were waiting for a bull to get up when I felt a puff of the breeze on the back of my neck.

Instantly all the buffalo were on their feet. Fritz's .350 roared and then everything was hidden in a cloud of dust as the herd stampeded. Eventually the dust cleared to reveal a buffalo bull sitting on his haunches like a huge dog. A shot behind the ear finished it. As we approached the downed bull, the rest of the herd moved off about 70 yards, stopped and swung around to stare at us, advanced a few paces, and stared again. There were several good bulls in the herd, but the animals were all packed so tightly together that I dared not shoot for fear of wounding a second beast.

That evening we hunted out from camp on foot. We saw good

numbers of oryx and zebra, both Grevy's and common, but nothing of much interest until we came upon two rhino, a cow with its almost full-grown calf. They were 100 yards away on the other side of a deep gully, so Joe suggested we give them our wind to see what they would do. When there was no reaction we began to shout rudely at them. That got their attention. They ran round in circles snorting like steam locomotives until they caught our scent, when they immediately started across the gully, apparently meaning to come over and teach us our manners. I put a bullet into the ground in front of the leader, close enough to spray its face with dust and gravel. It stopped so suddenly I thought I must have hit it, but came on again and was not discouraged until I fired a second shot. As they made off we saw that the cow was minus half its tail.

Midmorning the next day found us on a ridge, crouched behind a leafless bush, waiting, as a herd of buffalo drifted toward us. They were being pushed by a group of elephant that were feeding along behind and I still retain a clear memory of one of the cow elephants rather pointedly using one tusk to nudge a buffalo out of her way. Down to our right was a rhino standing under a tree and another with a calf had crossed the ridge behind us. The buffalo were almost within range when the wind shifted. The elephants' trunks went up like periscopes, then everything turned and poured down off the ridge like a waterfall. Everything, that is, but the solitary rhino. It was still standing under its tree as we ran by, turning its head from side to side as if bewildered by all the mad dashing about in the midday sun.

The buffalo milled around for a bit down in the valley, allowing me to get ahead of them and cut them off as they came over a saddle on the next ridge. The first one stopped to stare when it became aware of me. It had fairly wide horns and what appeared to be good bosses, so I hammered it. The rest of the herd thundered by, leaving it still standing there. I pumped two more shots into it and down it went. I was quite elated until I got up to it and discovered that the supposed horn bosses were merely plastered mud, and that my victim was an ancient, toothless cow! I was ragged unmercifully about that, of course, and Joe named the feature "Finn's Folly Ridge".

We took Kitibo, one of Joe's men, out to help bring in some of the meat. When we got back we found the other chap, Makewa, high up in a tree with my loaded 8x60 mm rifle in his hands. A large, spotted, long-legged wild animal with a long tail and big teeth had come almost into camp, he said. It was most likely a cheetah. It is easy to imagine that all native Africans are thoroughly familiar with their wild fauna, but that is far from being the case. Makewa had lived all his life in a densely populated district and had never seen so much as a zebra or giraffe before he came on this safari.

Later we had to go in to Barsalinga, about five miles away, to get tobacco for Kitibo. The village consisted of one ramshackle, mud and wattle *duka* (store) with a corrugated iron roof. In addition to tobacco, snuff, and packets of "10 Centi" cigarettes, it stocked blankets, tea and sugar, salt, corn meal and a vile brand of sickeningly sweet soda pop much favored by the local people. On the way home Joe stalked and shot a fine Grevy's zebra stallion with his 9.3x62 mm Mauser. He was using the standard DWM ammunition with 285-gr. soft-nose bullets at 2,360 fps muzzle velocity and he had to shoot his zebra twice because the first bullet blew up on its shoulder, opening a large surface wound but failing to penetrate into the chest. I believe that particular bullet must have been faulty, perhaps with a crack in its jacket, as otherwise that load always worked very reliably on thin-skinned game of all kinds.

Another morning we hunted upstream towards the balanced rock and quickly found tracks where buffalo had drunk during the night. While following them up we became aware of a most peculiar, loud, roaring noise. Investigation revealed two big impala bucks engaged in a furious fight. They crashed together with their heads low and pushed while at the same time trying to twist each other off balance with their interlocked horns. Several junior bucks looked on, but the does were feeding in seeming indifference. In the end one of the rivals had enough. It received a jab in the hindquarters as it broke away and was then chased out of sight by the victor.

The day was already hot when we caught up with the buffalo and they were bedded down in thick brush. Joe and I went in ahead and soon spotted the horns of two recumbent bulls. Beyond them a cow was moving around with its head hanging as if it were half asleep. We crawled up to a little tree and from there could see that one of the bulls was quite decent. Joe shot and the bull rolled over on its side. But, as I ran past it in pursuit of the herd it began to kick as if trying to get up, and I heard Joe shout to Fritz to come and finish it off for him, as he did not want to use any more of his precious hoard of .450 cartridges than were absolutely needed.

I pursued the herd for a while, but none of its members showed any inclination to stop and look back. Then they turned downwind and headed directly for the river and the game reserve beyond it, so I left them.

Joe and Fritz had to get back to their jobs, but I could take a few more days. I returned them to Isiolo and the Volkswagen, then with Kitibo, a cheerful and willing Kamba tribesman who had poached his share of meat with bow and poisoned arrows, I drove to the Shaffa Dinka area, some miles downstream from the bridge where the Marsabit road crossed the Uaso Nyiro (and in what much later became the Shaba Game Reserve), to see what might be accomplished there. In the afternoon we stopped at an encampment of Boran cattle herders and asked about buffalo. A young chap said he knew a place where they often lay up and volunteered to take us there. He led us down towards the river and, after some searching, we spotted a small herd in a palm thicket.

We crept up to it, and when I parted some fronds there, standing nicely broadside-on not 30 yards away, was a big, very black bull. Its horns looked enormous to my inexperienced eyes. Beyond it were a few cows and calves and a smaller bull. One of the cows was directly in line with the big fellow, so to avoid any chance of wounding it if the bullet should shoot completely through the bull, I decided to crawl a few yards to another gap in the palms. As I sat up to shoot a cow, unnoticed earlier, started to run. It came between me and the bull, the whole mob stampeded and that was that.

I was sadly disappointed and angry with myself for muffing a perfect opportunity, but the Boran cheerfully declared that there were many more buffalo. At first light next morning he took me to a place on the river where they often came to drink. Here we found fresh tracks and, after a short follow-up, came on the buffalo grazing slowly along. But the stalk was ruined by half-a-dozen waterbuck that caught our scent and ran straight towards the buffalo.

We stayed on the spoor and after some hours caught up with them again in an area of thorn brush. The fitful breeze was inconstant in the extreme and gave us away several times, but the buffalo wanted to bed down and did not go far. Once a cow with a very young calf got up from a clump of palmettos 20 yards away and came towards us. She peered suspiciously at the bush under which we crouched, came closer and stared again. I remembered Kipling's dictum, that "...the female of the species is more deadly than the male," and reflected that it was likely to be doubly true when she perceived a possible threat to her offspring. With the .375 in my hands I was confident that I could handle any trouble the cow might bring, but I desperately wanted to avoid having to shoot it. We sat absolutely still, trying not even to blink and at long last she went away, but took the herd with her. And so it went.

We had finally given up and were walking back along a ridge top towards the distant Land Rover, hot, weary and thirsty, when I saw another lot of buffalo below us. We made a stalk and were nearly within range when the accursed wind betrayed us again. Far more in anger than in hope I rushed after the buffalo and then realized that they were just trotting along. I put on a spurt and had closed to within 50 yards when two of them stopped and turned to look back. One of the pair was a bull and at that point I no longer cared. Big or small, any bull would do. So I flung up the .375 and shot for its shoulder. As the bullet smacked home the buffalo bucked and turned, and was gone in the brush before I could shoot again. But I found gouts of bright red, frothy, lung blood, and the bull was down and dead less than 60 paces away.

It was a small-bodied beast and although the horns were well-formed and had good bosses, they were small also. However, it was my first trophy buffalo and I was entirely delighted with it. I kept the head for a good number of years, though I no longer have it.

In truth, most of the trophies we collected on that trip have long since been discarded, and only my diary and the memories remain. Nevertheless, it was an unforgettable hunt, one that I will take pleasure in recalling the rest of my life.

18

Homecoming

Early in May 1977, I went down to a hunting block between Konza and the Athi River, not 30 miles from our home on the outskirts of Nairobi, seeking meat for our nearly empty freezer. The long rains had recently broken a protracted drought, and the Athi Plains were green, fresh and studded with wild flowers. When I signed in at the game department post at Athi River the game scouts there asked me to shoot a Grant's gazelle for them. I protested that I did not have a license for a Grant's, but they said that did not matter, it would not count.

Not far into the block I spotted a herd of 30 or 40 wildebeest. They are odd-looking animals with buffalo-like horns, white beards, horse-like manes, gray, sloping bodies brindled with darker stripes and long, flowing tails (which make excellent fly whisks). Appearances to the contrary, wildebeest are true antelopes, related to the hartebeests. They are quite crazy, liable to gallop off in all directions for no discernable reason at all, and then to wheel around and come back, or to suddenly stop and calmly start grazing as if nothing had happened. In this respect they remind one somewhat of caribou. They are also much the same size as caribou and their meat is every bit as tasty.

There was little cover, but finally by making use of shallow folds in the terrain I managed to get ahead of them and let them

189

move slowly past me at a range of about 200 yards. I sat down with the 7x64 mm Mauser, waited until a dry cow that I had been watching appeared to be in the clear on the fringe of the bunch, and fired. At the shot the cow ran, while another that must have been exactly in line beyond it staggered and went down. The second animal was still kicking, so I gave it a finisher, and then found the first one dead a little distance away. The 173-gr. RWS H-mantel (partition-type) bullet had passed completely through the first *gnu*, close behind its front legs (which was a little farther back than I had meant to place the shot) and had then struck the second in almost exactly the same spot. I had taken two impala with a single shot on several occasions previously, but this was the first time I experienced it with wildebeest. It was quite unintentional, but it did not matter as I had tags for two wildebeest and had meant to fill them in any case.

I spent a couple of hours skinning and cutting up the wildebeest and loading them into the Toyota and then went after a *granti* for the game scouts. I found some on absolutely flat ground where there was no possibility of making a stalk, so just walked openly and casually obliquely towards them, until at last they had let me close to within about 150 yards. There I knelt, to get as low and steady as possible and still be able to see over the tall grass, and dropped one of the gazelles in its tracks. It was the last shot I fired in my native land.

Two weeks later we were visiting some friends at Karatina (not far from Mt. Kenya) planning a hunt on which Berit would try for a buffalo, when our host came in and put the newspaper down on the breakfast table in front of me.

"HUNTING BANNED" proclaimed the headlines. "Directive to Save Wildlife. All game hunting has been banned in Kenya. All hunting licenses have been canceled and all hunting safaris have been told to stop — at once. Announcing the ban yesterday, Tourism and Wildlife Minister Mr. Mathew Ogutu said 'There are no exceptions...the ban is indefinite'...Mr.Ogutu said

190

A HUNTER REMEMBERS

the Firearms Bureau had been told to cancel all licenses for hunting weapons immediately...Mr.Ogutu said the Government would lose 10 million shillings a year from hunting license revenues...He assured that hunters whose licenses were canceled would get their money back." (I am still waiting for it.)

Kenya's populations of elephant, rhino, leopard and, to some extent, zebra were being wiped out by poachers, there was no question about that. For years the price of ivory had held steady at about three U.S. dollars per pound and license fees were set accordingly, so that the ivory from a 50-pounder would just about cover the costs. There was a little poaching, mainly by tribesmen using bows and poisoned arrows, but it was no problem. The chief threat came from Kenya's explosive population growth; settlement and cultivation were rapidly encroaching on the elephants' remaining habitat and many hundreds had to be shot by the game department in defense of crops every year, while in Tsavo National Park thousands more died of starvation.

Then, in the early 1970s, the price of ivory on the international market started to rise. It doubled and quadrupled and went still higher (it stood at about $100 per pound when the international accord against the importation of ivory was signed in 1990), and then the dam burst. Bushmen with their primitive bows were replaced by organized gangs of poachers (many of them from Somalia) armed with modern rifles, including fully automatic military weapons, who wiped out whole families of elephant at a time and swept the country clean of rhino, and who had sufficient determination and firepower to overwhelm the underpaid game department and national park scouts, armed only with obsolete Mark III .303 Lee-Enfields.

To compound the mess, several powerful members of the ruling hierarchy were most profitably involved in the buying and exporting of poached ivory and could not be touched. The Nairobi police once stopped and impounded a truck-full of undocumented ivory and threw the driver into the pokey.

191

AAGAARD'S AFRICA

Within the hour an order came down from on high: turn the driver loose, give him back the truck and the ivory, and delete all mention of the incident from the records.

Ostensibly to regain control of the situation, and in response to the rising tide of criticism both at home and from abroad, the Government banned legal, licensed hunting. They banned an activity that gainfully employed several thousand Kenyans and brought in better than six million dollars in desperately needed foreign exchange every year while taking only 6,000 animals of all species a season. (In comparison, three times that many whitetail are harvested yearly in Llano County, Texas, where I now live.) As a result, the elephant population in Kenya, which stood at over 65,000 animals at the time of the hunting ban, had been reduced to a mere 17,000 by 1989 and is still steadily declining. Such is the logic of governments.

Interestingly enough, Kenya's parliament was not consulted before the ban on hunting was proclaimed and no free debate on the issue was permitted. Under the British colonial regime the law had been written with the convenience of the bureaucracy very much in mind. The chief game warden was given the power to revoke anyone's game license at any time, without having to give any explanation or justification. This worked well enough so long as the incumbent had a deeply ingrained sense of fair play, but it was obviously open to abuse. Be that as it may, the Kenya Government was able to impose the hunting ban immediately and without any public discussion, by simply ordering the chief game warden to revoke all hunting licenses. The lesson should be obvious.

I put the newspaper down, got up and walked out onto the veranda in a slight state of shock. Alright, we would have to cancel the safaris we had booked and return the deposits. We might fill in to some extent with photographic safaris, although they bored me, and we could extend our farming enterprise. Even now Berit was doing quite well from our five-acre plot. She sold the milk from our two jersey cows, eggs from 200 hens and

192

vegetables from the garden to the embassies and expatriate communities in Nairobi, and was supplying ducks to one popular restaurant. If we obtained a little more land we might make something out of that. On the other hand, did I really want to stay in the sort of country Kenya was becoming, and in a place where I could not occasionally go out and hunt for myself? More to the point, could I consent to being disarmed, and to having to live in Africa with no effective means of protecting myself and my family?

I turned to Berit and said, "That's it. We are leaving."

I wrote to everyone I knew in the United States, most of whom were former clients. Ever since my schooldays I had admired and been convinced of the truth of the ideals on which America was founded and was, as I still am, a fervent supporter of the Constitution and the Bill of Rights. Dunlop Farren in Houston, Texas, (who with his wife, Sue, had hunted with me the previous year) proved to be a true friend when we needed one and what we owe him we can never adequately repay. He found me a job with an exotic game operation near Kerrville that would qualify us to enter the country as permanent residents, and then spent untold hours shepherding the application through all the byways and detours of the bureaucratic process. In the fall of 1978, a year and a half after the hunting ban was imposed, the Aagaard family, lock, stock and barrel, arrived in the United States of America.

The exotic game hunting concern was a put-and-take, guaranteed-kill type of operation and not exactly my style. But while working for them I was sent a couple of times to guide hunters on a 7,000-acre ranch near Llano, in the Texas Hill Country, where the exotics were not fenced in or fed, but were completely free-ranging and lived as naturally as the numerous, native whitetail deer. I suggested to my boss that in addition to the guaranteed-kill type of hunting, we should offer fair chase hunts on foot on this property, but he could not see it. When I asked if I could pursue the matter, he said that it would be OK.

AAGAARD'S AFRICA

The upshot was that I made arrangements with Dr. Buttery, the present owner, to live in the huge old ranch house (with a hallway 25 yards long and sufficient room to put up all the clients I could handle at one time) and to take over the exotic game hunting on his Bar-O Ranch. The property had previously belonged to the Moss family, whose ancestors had been granted land in this area for service in the Texas revolution. Mark A. Moss had started to stock exotic game on it around the time of World War II. Exactly when the various species were introduced I could not determine, but the aoudad (Barbary sheep) were established in huntable numbers by 1945 and Herb Klein, writing in Mellon's *African Hunter*, recorded killing one on this ranch while hunting mouflon here in that year. I also received permission to hunt exotics on the neighboring Inks Ranch (whose owner, Jim Inks, is a nephew of Mark A. Moss) and some others, including the Greenwood Valley Ranch near Rocksprings with its abundant axis deer.

For nine years I guided hunters here for a living, allowing nothing but strictly fair-chase hunts whereby the game was stalked on foot. I started writing on the side and then George Martin, the Executive Director of Publications for the National Rifle Association, offered me a contract to write exclusively for the NRA, which I was proud to accept. In 1988 I closed down the guiding business in order to write full-time, but we continue to live in the old ranch house and keep an eye on the exotic game. In the meantime Berit went back to school, and qualified first as a Licensed Vocational Nurse and then, after two hard years of driving two hours each way to classes, as a Registered Nurse.

Llano, on the Llano River, is a pretty little town of 3,000 good folks, 75 miles west of Austin, the closest city of any size. It is a solid town, too, with a sense of community and pride in itself. The small hospital is excellent and so are the schools, where discipline is still administered with a paddle when that is necessary. The marching band does outstandingly well in state competitions and even the football team enjoys consistent

194

winning seasons. It has been a wholesome environment in which to raise a family.

The country looks a great deal like some parts of Kenya. It is mainly open oak and mesquite woodland, with occasional stands of elm and hickory, and big pecan trees along the watercourses. In places the sweet-smelling bee brush grows thick and prickly pear is widespread. Mustang grapes, which make delicious jelly, grow wild. The terrain is hilly, with fantastic granite outcrops and rocky ridges, and there is little arable land. This is ranching country; cattle, angora goats and some sheep. And it is a place for wild turkeys and whitetail deer, more whitetail deer per square mile than almost anywhere else on earth.

The deer are small, but exceedingly abundant. I have come to love them and would not again very willingly live where I did not have them around me. Most of the deer hunting on the ranch is leased out on a permanent basis. Some of the hunters have been coming every season for the past 30 years and more, and now their grandchildren hunt here as well. A few of the smaller, but still amply spacious, pastures are not leased out and there we are permitted to collect our venison. We hunt whitetail in season by simply picking up a rifle and walking out from the house far enough to avoid killing the home deer and then we still-hunt. As in Kenya, almost all the meat we eat is a product of the rifle.

My shooting bench is by the creek, not 100 yards from the house, which makes load development in particular very convenient. It is shaded by a huge, ancient live-oak tree and a big pecan that yields quantities of excellent nuts, most of which the squirrels get, just as they get all the fruit from the pear tree outside the kitchen window.

We share this ramshackle, near century-old house with many different creatures. The armadillos root in its lawn and flower beds, and bang and rattle against the hodgepodge of plumbing under its floor when they come in at night. Squirrels scamper about the attic and grow fat sprawled out on the bird table, where they are just as entertaining as the birds. A courageous and busy little wren raised her young on a shelf in my daughter's bedroom between two Cabbage Patch Dolls, and a phoebe insists on building her nest every year around the light that hangs on the porch outside the front door. Hummingbirds buzz and strafe each other at the feeders all summer long, while at least a dozen glowing cardinals brighten the yard. The mud-dauber wasps litter the porch with paralyzed black widow spiders and cause me to plug with bullets the muzzles of the guns we keep openly displayed in a rack. A colony of harvester ants lives by the corner of the porch. They cut the leaves from the pear tree, unless I sprinkle Sevin dust around it, and all day a stream of them marches home, laden with cracked corn and seeds from the bird table. Two tremulous cottontails nervously nibble at the grain the careless squirrels spill, and at night a plump racoon comes to clean up whatever the ants, birds, rabbits and squirrels have left. There is no provision for locking the doors of the house, nor is there any need to do so.

Nearly every evening I go for a brisk, one-hour walk and, if she is home, Berit accompanies me. Often I'll take a pistol along and, where the backstop is safe, fire a magazine- or cylinder-full or two at cactus pads to help keep my eye in — it needs all the help it can get. We always see some wildlife: aoudad, feral hogs, axis, sika or fallow deer and I cannot remember the last time we failed to put up a whitetail, usually we see at least a dozen of them. Our way of life is essentially the same as it was on the Yatta and at Juja Farm. I do not know of a better place in the world to live and I believe that at long last I have come home.